ALL YOUR WAVES SWEPT OVER ME

Looking for God in Natural Disasters

Edited by
**Nancy de Flon and
James A. Wallace, CSsR**

Paulist Press
New York/Mahwah, NJ

Cover design by Sharyn Banks
Book design by Lynn Else

Library of Congress Cataloging-in-Publication Data

All your waves swept over me : looking for God in natural disasters / edited by Nancy de Flon and James A. Wallace.
    p. cm.
    Includes bibliographical references.
    ISBN-13: 978-0-8091-4502-7 (alk. paper)
    1. Natural disasters—Religious aspects—Christianity. I. De Flon, Nancy Marie. II. Wallace, James A.
BT161.A45 2007
231′.8—dc22

                          2007020810

Published by Paulist Press
997 Macarthur Boulevard
Mahwah, New Jersey 07430

www.paulistpress.com

Printed and bound in the
United States of America

Contents

Foreword

Antoinette Bosco

The first time I was ever aware of the impact of a "natural disaster" was in the late 1930s when I was still in elementary school. I had gone to the movies with my mother, who wanted to see a film called *Hurricane,* which was getting great reviews. At that stage in life, I was much too young to have yet become aware of the kind of monumental disaster that can hit our world. But as I watched this movie, I learned.

Yet, when I left the theater, I was not focusing on the horror of the hurricane that hit innocent island people. I was still thinking of the movie's end. As people tried to leave their island to escape the falling trees and earthly devastation, they had only one way to do this—via small boats. On one of the boats was a young pregnant woman in labor, with an older woman trying to help her. As the storm finally subsided, there was a cry—the wail of a newborn baby. All the people on the boat soared with joy for the new life that had survived the disaster.

I asked my mother, "Was that a miracle?" And she answered, "Yes, of course," and added something to the effect that no matter what happens, nothing can stop the love of God that comes to us every time when a baby is born.

I never forgot those words from my mother, who probably had no idea that she had just given her young child a lifelong lesson about where God is when a terrible disaster hits his earth and his people. God is busy being God—the One who never stops giving life to his creation.

Of course, this was a lesson I had to learn over and over in the years ahead as I often became confused about God. This was true especially when I learned of historical disasters that had no apparent explanation, like the lost continent of Atlantis; the burying of Pompeii by the poisonous lava of a volcano; the San Francisco earthquake; and so many more up to the present day, like the 2004 tsunami disaster, Hurricane Katrina, and the Pakistan/India earthquakes.

Foreword

All these disasters may have different, and even explainable, causes. Yet they raise one common set of questions: Where is God when the earth erupts, causing such pain to his children? Why didn't God create a perfectly running world? How can we make sense out of something that appears to make no sense?

These questions are very old. They were raised long ago, when suffering Job shook his fist at God and asked his "Why's" for having been afflicted with multiple disasters. God responded with a "Wow!"—giving him a remarkable answer that began with a surprising rebuke, reminding Job that he was not the One who had set "the cornerstone of the universe." Job wanted answers, and God said, "No way," because to understand them, Job would have to be God-sized—and that was neither possible nor recommended.

Father Ronald Rolheiser expresses this well: "We cannot see the whole picture; the gap between the infinite and the finite cannot be bridged by understanding, but only by faith and wonder."

Anyone who has studied science would have to agree that we don't know "the whole picture." Scientists now talk about "nonlinearity," the idea that it's chaos out there in the universe. What it comes down to is that we don't live in a nice, neat world. Think of the asymmetry of cloud shapes, the jagged edge of a lightning bolt, the branching of a tree or river. This is nature flowing freely and unpredictably and—I have to believe from eternity's perspective—beautifully. The recent scientific theories of chaos and irregularity in the universe suggest to me that if God throws us a curve ball, he must have his reasons for this, even if we can't understand them at the moment. Maybe our mysterious Creator never wanted us to be deluded into thinking we could have God all figured out!

John Polkinghorne, an Anglican priest and scientist, maintains that we must still deal with mystery because the world is not finished but evolving. "No doubt God could have created everything ready-made, if that is what he had wanted to do. In fact, however, he has chosen to do something cleverer than that. An evolutionary world is to be understood theologically as a world allowed by its Creator to make itself."

That is a good explanation for why all that is earthly is far from perfect. We can't yet answer what chaos in creation means, though scientists are beginning to find glimmers of understanding from researching what is being called "the emerging science of complexity." In 1992 physicist Dr. George F. Smoot reported a cosmic discovery linked to the big bang that was a true example of this. He said he found "ripples" in space that presumably were the seeds that blossomed into stars, planets, and people. His comment on this discovery was noteworthy, and stories on his findings were printed not just in scientific journals but also in the major newspapers. "It is a mystical experience," he said. "It really is like finding the driving mechanism for the universe, and isn't that what God is?"

Meanwhile, we all live with our feet on earth's ground and so can relate to events in the here and now—like earthquakes, hurricanes, volcanic eruptions, and floods—that confuse and sadden us: we've got them in multiples. We see danger when nature goes on the wild side, the rains roar and the volcanoes erupt; we see tears when a living, beloved person has a body overcome by an illness or disease; we see traumatic pain when death comes suddenly and unnaturally. For me this is personal, for I'll never know why three of my sons had to die, one by suicide, one by murder, one by heart failure.

We live in a world of mystery. We don't know why there is pain and death any more than we know why this world has to have natural disasters. But likewise, we don't know why there is sunlight and food and love, and babies who do grow into strong adults and live to do good in this world. I have come to believe that if we want to shake a fist at God because he didn't prevent pain, we've lost our way; we want to redefine God, turning him into some kind of cosmic bellhop who brings us what we want and caters to our requests to make us comfortable. A very respected Presbyterian minister, Frederick Buechner, once underscored, "A clenched fist can't accept anything."

I found wisdom and comfort in the words of Father Rolheiser in his book *The Shattered Lantern,* and I pass these on: "God does not start fires, or floods, or wars, or AIDS, or anything else of this nature in order to wake us up and bring us back to true values. Nature, chance, human freedom, and human sin bring these things to pass. However, to say that God does not initiate or cause these things is not the same thing as saying that God does not speak through them. God is in these chance events, both the disastrous ones and in the advantageous ones, and speaks through them."

His words brought me back to my childhood, the hurricane movie, its ending, and the lesson I learned from my mother's words. Yes, there is disaster, pain, sorrow, and death, but there is, above all, God, who continually gives life to his creation.

Foreword

Admittedly, as human beings, we always want answers, never more crucially than when a natural disaster hits with uncountable, gigantic loss. The chapters that follow will open doors. Walk in and listen to what these fine scholars and students of the Lord have learned from their own studies about how we find God in natural disasters that take a toll in lives, property, nurturing, and, too often, faith.

Brookfield, Connecticut

Preface

Anyone who regularly reads or listens to the news must inevitably reach this conclusion: Natural disasters are here to stay. Hurricanes, tsunamis, tornadoes—the entire repertoire of destructive events that nature can stage for our dismay and devastation—have established themselves as permanent features in our landscape.

As long as individuals, corporations, and countries continue to disregard the importance of working in harmony with nature in favor of greedily exploiting it for consumerism and profit, nature will take revenge and people will end up as bit players in one of The Weather Channel's *Storm Stories*. And as long as outdoor enthusiasts insert themselves into face-to-face encounters with nature's elemental forces without sufficient respect and preparation for the destructive potential of these forces, they will end up as protagonists in an adventure tale of extreme survival at best or, at worst, as fatal statistics in a mountaineering organization's annual accident reports.

Inevitably, in the wake of natural disasters, especially those of such overwhelming magnitude as the December 2004 tsunami or the hurricanes of 2005, there emerges the usual rash of commentators eager to offer their answers to the question that haunts most people at these times: "Where was God when this happened?" Unfortunately, it appears, as a general rule, that the commentators' eagerness to express their opinion is in inverse proportion to the value of what they have to say.

Convinced that more responsible voices need to be heard in this context, we have invited a group of intelligent and educated Catholics to reflect on looking for God in natural disasters. Each contributor writes from within the context of his or her own discipline.

Dolores R. Leckey ("Landscapes and Inscapes") invites a host of friends into the conversation—including John Polkinghorne, Elie Wiesel, and a young woman named Margaret—to help her articulate her own deeply personal and spiritual response to nature's less-pretty side.

Kevin J. O'Neil, CSsR ("What's God Got to Do with It? Natural Disasters and Moral Agency"), challenges the notion of God as a moral agent in natural disasters, and asks provocative questions about human responsibility in such events.

Dianne Bergant, CSA ("Out of the Depths I Cry to You, O LORD"), probes relevant scriptural passages for questions about tragedies of nature as manifestations of an angry God.

Francis J. Moloney, SDB ("God Is Watching Us—From a Distance"), considers the scriptural themes of sin, evil, grace, and blessing as his basis for reflecting on the interaction between the Creator God and God's creation.

Richard E. McCarron ("Why Have You Abandoned Us? Liturgy in Time of Natural Disaster") looks at the vital role played by prayer and worship, both formal and informal, as response to natural disasters, and offers a model for a liturgy that can be adapted and used in such a context.

James A. Wallace, CSsR ("Preaching in the Face of Natural Disasters"), offers suggestions for how someone faced with preaching in the aftermath of a catastrophic natural event might respond to the myriad anguished questions that inevitably surface at such tragic times.

John Vidmar, OP ("Plague, Famine, Yellow Fever: Religious Repercussions of Three Natural Disasters"), turns a historian's lens on the Black Death, the Irish Potato Famine, and the yellow-fever epidemic in Tennessee, to focus on responses by the official church and the average Catholic.

Nancy de Flon ("Looking at Nature 'From Both Sides Now'") brings a variety of creative artists, nature writers, and outdoor adventurers into a conversation about multifaceted nature and the ultimately mysterious God who created and cares for it.

Robert Béla Wilhelm ("Appreciating the Beauty: A Traditional Hawaiian Tale") uses a Hawaiian folk-story to talk about human alienation from, and reconciliation with, the rest of God's creation.

We hope that the voices in this book offer you a worthy alternative to the doomsayers, pseudo-theological pundits, and purveyors of pious platitudes who would each have you believe that they possess the Whole Truth about where God is operative in natural disasters. It is our wish that we will have led you to a deeper appreciation of, and awe before, God's countless ways of being in touch with "the work of his hands" (Psalm 19) even in the worst of times.

Nancy de Flon, PhD
Ramsey, New Jersey

James A. Wallace, CSsR
Washington Theological Union

Contributors

Dianne Bergant, CSA, is professor of biblical studies at Catholic Theological Union in Chicago. She is the author of several books on biblical themes and is presently the Old Testament book reviewer of *The Bible Today*. She is currently working in the areas of biblical interpretation and biblical theology, particularly issues of peace, ecology, and feminism.

Antoinette Bosco is a syndicated columnist for Catholic News Service in Washington, DC, and the author of fifteen books. A mother of seven, of whom three are deceased, she pursues a personal ministry of helping people who are hurting from the painful loss of a loved one. She is also active in prison ministry work.

Nancy de Flon, who holds a PhD in church history from Union Theological Seminary in New York, is an editor at Paulist Press and coauthor, with John Vidmar, OP, of *101 Questions and Answers on* The Da Vinci Code *and the Catholic Tradition* (Paulist Press, 2006). An avid hiker and photographer, she has researched and given talks on religious themes in the art of the Hudson River School.

Dolores R. Leckey has been a senior fellow at the Woodstock Theological Center, Georgetown University, since 1998. Prior to that, she was executive director of the Secretariat for Laity, Family, Women, and Youth of the USCCB. She is the author of a dozen books, the most recent being *Laity and Christian Education* (2006) in the Paulist Press series Rediscovering Vatican II.

Richard E. McCarron, PhD, is associate professor of liturgy at Catholic Theological Union in Chicago. He is the author of *The Eucharistic Prayer at Sunday Mass* (Liturgy Training Publications, 1997) and currently coeditor of *New Theology Review*.

Contributors

Francis J. Moloney, SDB, a senior New Testament scholar, recently served as the Katharine Drexel Professor of Religious Studies, and the dean of the School of Theology, at the Catholic University of America, Washington, DC. He is currently the provincial superior of the Salesians of Don Bosco in Australia and the Pacific.

Kevin J. O'Neil, CSsR, is associate professor of moral theology at the Washington Theological Union and coauthor of *The Essential Moral Handbook* (Liguori, 2006) and *Educating Leaders for Ministry* (Liturgical Press, 2005).

John Vidmar, OP, holds an STD from the Angelicum in Rome. He is the archivist of the Dominican Province of St. Joseph; an associate professor of theology at Providence College in Providence, Rhode Island; author of *The Catholic Church Through the Ages;* and coauthor, with Nancy de Flon, of *101 Questions and Answers on* The Da Vinci Code *and the Catholic Tradition* (both published by Paulist Press, 2005 and 2006).

James A. Wallace, CSsR, is professor of homiletics at the Washington Theological Union, and served as president of the Academy of Homiletics (2005). His publications include *Preaching to the Hungers of the Heart* (Liturgical Press, 2002) and the three-book series and the three-book series *Lift Up Your Hearts: Homilies and Reflections for the "A" Cycle* [2004]; *"B" Cycle* [2006]; and *"C" Cycle* [2006], all with Guerric DeBona, OSB, and the late Robert P. Waznak, SS (Paulist Press).

Robert Béla Wilhelm, ThD, is the founder and director of the School of Sacred Storytelling at www.sacredstorytelling.org and heads Storyfest Journeys and Pilgrimages at www.storyfest.com.

1

Landscapes and Inscapes
Dolores R. Leckey

May the glory of the LORD endure forever;
    may the LORD rejoice in his works—
who looks on the earth and it trembles,
    who touches the mountains and they smoke.
I will sing to the LORD as long as I live;
    I will sing praise to my God while I have being.
                                    Psalm 104:31–33

The psalms are filled with fierce floods and exploding mountains, and still the psalmist manages to hold on to a recurring theme: "I will sing praise to the Lord while I live." That determination stands out like a path to the inner world, and it orders the "inscape," no matter that natural disasters sweep through our landscapes.

Personal Experience

I have little firsthand experience of natural disasters. A couple of times I was in the "almost" category. There was the time I landed at Tampa International Airport in the midst of a huge storm that had no name. It was not classified as a hurricane, but visibility disappeared, the airport was closed, the wind raged, and street signs were flying around. I'm sure I prayed as I waited in disbelief that I was actually in such an unpredictable situation. It was impossible to drive so I waited until there was a lull that came eventually, enabling me to proceed to my brother's safe and secure home, prayers of gratitude encircling my mind and heart.

And I have had occasional brushes with real *named* hurricanes, usually in late summer. When announcements shift from watching to

1

warning, I do the usual things: fill the bathtub with water, and check for candles and flashlights and household supplies. Once my basement was flooded right up to the kitchen door, furnace floating about and basement walls later covered with mud. I, however, was in the hospital at the time, giving birth to my fourth child, and so I missed all the anguish and aftermath.

Another time I was driving in Maine with several of my children. Tom was about eight years old, and when we heard on the car radio that a tornado was spotted on the road we were traveling, Tom told me to turn right. Why? I wanted to know. He said tornadoes cannot make right turns (or left, I suppose). Where did he learn this? I asked. In school, he told me. My confidence in the Virginia educational system increased immediately. And I followed his directions.

So as I ponder the effects of nature at full force on both the landscapes and on personal inscapes of people's souls as they confront the resulting rearrangement and loss in their lives, I am drawn to the stories of others, both strangers and friends, my own being so limited. And I am drawn to imagining how being uprooted might eventually root one more deeply in God's abiding compassion.

Others' Experiences

Because of twenty-first-century technology, we are in touch with the fracturing of landscapes almost as it happens. Like millions of Americans I watched the unleashing of Katrina's strength, and its consequences, as that now-mythic hurricane washed over New Orleans, changing forever its famous profile. I thought of my friend Gretchen, a religious sister who was born and raised in New Orleans and who, as a Marianist of the Holy Cross, lives and ministers there. Only she wasn't there during Katrina (so I learned later); she was in France with her community. It was months before she could return to the city of her birth, the city that has always been her true home. She wrote me about her feelings: "I can remember yearning…for home. I remember thinking during December [2005] that perhaps this is what Advent is meant to be, *yearning* to be in our ultimate home." What she found when she finally arrived home, in January of 2006, was heartbreak. Now she is looking for the beauty in the brokenness. Gretchen is a woman of deep prayer with an eye to discover the hidden, so I trust she will find the beauty.

2

But still, there are questions that turn up in my inscape. What would I *actually* do if waves were to wash over me? I'm not a heroic type, I tend to avoid risky situations, I scare easily. I have always lived in a certain degree of comfort. I do, however, have confidence in prayer, which is an essential part of my everyday life. I think of myself as normal. And so I recently talked with another friend, living a "normal" life, who at age eighteen had lived through the 1954 hurricane named Carol.

Tim Wholey and his parents and siblings spent summers in Jerusalem, Rhode Island. He told me that the people in that small fishing village at first had no idea they were experiencing a hurricane. They thought it was a bad northeast storm, but when Tim and his brother Joe returned to their cottage after driving their father to the train station in Kingston, they had trouble holding the car to the road. The rain was tremendous, "biting like nails." The brothers glanced at the harbor and saw the dock roll up like a roll of wrapping paper. They thought they should try to drive to safety (they saw several cars ahead of them attempting the same thing), but the first car in the line stalled. A nurse they knew got out of her car and tried to push the car in front, but then the car disappeared in the waves. The nurse, seeking safety, ran to join the brothers in their car. A state trooper, en route to warn the people in the fishing village, drowned in the marshes. The people in the exodus, about thirty-five, realized they couldn't make it out of the village, so they gathered in what appeared to be the house highest from the water. Tim's mother was among them, and at one point she opened a window and threw a medal into the water, which by then had reached the porch. Cars and houses floated by as "the gathered" watched in wonder. With regularity, people would start prayers and all joined in. These prayers, remembers Tim, were positive, not prayers of fear, more like "I will sing praise to the Lord while I live." Tim thinks that because there were so many small children in the group, the adults were upbeat for them. He recalls one elderly woman going into a small bedroom and repeatedly saying the Rosary.

Writer Arthur Jones says that when we are most frightened, we cling tightest to God.

THE BEADS

Onyx, plastic, pearl and gold
The Beadsman a thousand Aves told.
I tell mine when the world feels cold.

3

Pay him a penny, pay him a groat
The Beadsman's thousand Aves: rote.
I finger mine in the bottom of my coat.
Plastic, pearl, gold and jade
The Beadsman a thousand Aves prayed.
I pray mine most when I'm afraid.
Pursed in leather, pocketed in cloth
I clutch mine tightest
when the plane takes off.

Arthur C. Jones

Tim's feeling at the time of Hurricane Carol was that "God knew of our dilemma, had indeed let it happen. Our fate was in God's hands; our prayers were heard." And in a small room an old woman kept "telling" her Aves. All those gathered in the house survived.

God's Will?

God let it happen, Tim said. An interesting comment. One often hears it in the form of a question. A Jesuit colleague, Fr. John Chathanatt, SJ, after a major Indian earthquake several years ago, wrote a column "Unshaken Faith" for the Indian newspaper *Indian Express* in which he asked: What is God doing? Father John framed his answer in much the same way as do scripture scholars; namely, look at the totality of the event, not at individual pieces. The totality of this particular earthquake included more than the number dead or the number of destroyed homes. It included the reactions of the victims, their support of one another, their courage, and the compassionate responses of the nation and the world. The earthquake released forces of love that went beyond duty. People experienced solidarity and even a form of conversion. They gathered in temples, mosques, and churches not out of despair, writes the Jesuit, but out of fellow feeling. Survivors and others then quickly analyzed the situation, bringing intellectual judgments into their experience of love. They wanted to remedy, as best they could, the problems at the root of the disaster. They knew they couldn't prevent future earthquakes but they could attend to building houses that would survive. The result would be that some people would receive better houses than before, and others would shift from palatial mansions to more modest structures. Not only did the populace then have safe dwellings, but the community rebuilt along more egalitarian lines. Father John wrote, "The earthquake did not discriminate on the basis of caste or religion.... All were treated equally." Relationships deepened, he observed, including the human relationship with God. So what *was* God doing? God was being God, and the human response in India was to praise God with intelligence and compassion, recognizing that grace abounds even in earthquakes.

Continuing Creation

It seems to me that we can gain some insight into God being God through the efforts of theologians working at the borders of science. John Polkinghorne, for example, who is both scientist and priest-theologian, continues to illuminate—for ordinary normal Christian believers like me—the rationality present in the divine relationship with creation. He and others hold up what might be called a theology of nature: that God allows the created other to be itself. And so the earth's plate tectonics whose constant movement creates mountains and valleys also cause some of those mountains to spew forth volcanic ash, or the earth to tremble as the crust adjusts, or the sea to rise up to great heights. I recently heard a rabbi embrace this view, saying that the Hebrew word that we translate as "creation" is really, in Hebrew, "becoming." So rather than thinking of creation as static and finished, a faithful Hebrew translation presents creation as dynamic.

In his book *Science and the Trinity*, Polkinghorne points to the eightfold reiteration in Genesis that nothing exists except through the creative will and effectual utterance of God. *And God said, let there be...* One can almost hear the utterances reverberating through time and through all created life, including human life, including the Word becoming flesh in the person of Jesus. And it is this event, the incarnation, in which God truly shares to the uttermost in the travail of creation. Theologian Jürgen Moltmann's understanding is that the Christian God is not a compassionate spectator of the suffering creatures, but the crucified God who is truly the fellow sufferer who understands, the One who is a partner in pain.

5

What was God doing during the 2004 tsunami, the Indian and Pakistani earthquakes, and Hurricane Katrina? I think the theologian-scientists are right: God was a fellow sufferer. This is the same insight offered by Elie Wiesel in his memoir *Night* about the horrors of the Holocaust. A question that has long haunted believers and nonbelievers is, "Where was God when Jews were being mercilessly slaughtered?" God was there, on the gallows, writes Wiesel. Or, as the son of a Holocaust survivor reflected, "God was within every Jew who told a story or a joke or sang a melody in a death camp barrack to alleviate a friend's agony" (quoted in my *7 Essentials for the Spiritual Journey*, 104).

Cocreating: Cooperation and Collaboration

Recognizing that many, perhaps most, natural disasters consist in the working-out of the creative utterances of God, another question logically arises: What is the extent of human responsibility in all of this? It is a question at the center of events like the Holocaust, not a *natural* disaster, but nonetheless a tragedy of incomprehensible proportions. It is possible to name the perpetrators who were responsible for the devastation, and to name the victims who exercised responsibility for preserving human dignity.

In Paul's Letter to the Romans (5:21), we read that where sin abounded, grace did more abound, Christ's presence being pervasive throughout the universe. This in no way limits human freedom, however. We can choose to disregard the grace that courses through life, or we can cooperate with it. In reflecting on God's presence in natural disasters, we must face the question of human responsibility in the landscapes of our world. Specifically, how is our Western lifestyle as consumers of carbon dioxide contributing to global warming and the consequent disasters?

For many decades now, there has been theological conversation about a growing consciousness among ordinary women and men that, in the course of their daily lives, they are participating in continuing creation. This new consciousness is being shaped through various practices of contemplation (or mindfulness), through commitment to ethical practice in work and civil life, through efforts to redress systemic injustice, and through explicit connection with others searching for more depth in their lives, either in spiritual direction/friendship relationships or faith-sharing groups of all kinds. These spiritual practices help people to sharpen their sense of responsibility for the world. Trends like these suggest a linkage between tending to our inner worlds and becoming ever more consciously responsible for the shape of our outer worlds; such trends also suggest a willingness to sacrifice in order to preserve the world. How do we do this?

Caring for the Inscapes

Praying with Others

John Polkinghorne, as a Christian believer and a scientist, points out that almost all believers in God are anchored in a particular faith-tradition. Their belief comes from the *experience* of worship and practice within a religious community as much as from, or more than, intellectual conviction and metaphysical reasoning. The implications are that we can look to our faith-traditions for the resources needed to care for our souls. First and foremost is to participate in worship with fellow believers on a regular basis. Certainly the three Abrahamic religions emphasize the centrality of gathering, of community. Islam requires its adherents to join with others at the mosque on Fridays; Jews are encouraged to be observant, which includes attendance at synagogue on Saturdays; Christians attend church on Sundays, coming together in remembrance of Jesus' death and resurrection in the breaking of bread and sharing of wine.

For Christians, their weekly gathering also presents them with the scriptural foundations of their belief system and explicitly links them to their Jewish heritage. Through psalms and Old Testament readings, in particular the Wisdom literature, we enter bit by bit into realization of what God is and what God does. In 1 Kings 19, for example, we follow Elijah in his flight from the wrath of Jezebel into the desert, where he is spent beyond all measure. Resting under a broom tree he prays for death, and then falls asleep. An angel appears, urging him to eat and drink, and indeed provisions appear. Elijah eats and sleeps, not displaying much energy until once again the angel of the Lord touches him and this time directs him not only to eat but to eat well in preparation for a long journey that awaits him. Elijah does as he is directed and then walks forty days and forty nights to Horeb, the mountain of God. There he enters a cave where he experiences the word of the Lord, which directs him further: "Go outside and stand on the mountain before the Lord; the Lord will be passing by." A strong and heavy wind rends the mountain and crushes the rocks, but the Lord is not in the wind. After the wind there is an earthquake, but the Lord is not in the earthquake. After the earthquake there is fire, but the Lord is not in the fire. After the fire there is a tiny whispering sound. When Elijah hears this, he hides his face in his cloak and goes and stands at the entrance to the cave. Some translations describe the whisper as "sheer silence."

In this narrative we see what God does—spectacular natural events, and earthquakes and fire—and who God is: the One beyond the fireworks, the One who is as close as the human heart. The Eastern churches are helpful here, making, as they do, a distinction between divine essence (God's being) and divine energies (God's activities). Even more helpful, I think, is Polkinghorne's insight that the act of creation is an act of divine kenosis involving self-limitation. It involves a kind of divine "making way" for the existence of the created order. God interacts with creatures, but does not overrule them. This clearly implies that not everything that happens (the act of a murderer or the incidence of cancer, for example) is brought about *directly* by God. God is emptying, allowing creatures to *be* themselves (*Science and the Trinity*, 84–85).

Week after week we are reminded of Jesus' image of God as *father*, and as the God of the living not the dead. (See Mark 12:18–28.) Week after week we listen to St. Paul's exhortation to *be* the Body of Christ. And every once in a while we experience it, not as an intellectual construct but as deep awareness, intuitive knowledge, something like Elijah at the entrance to the cave, steeped in the sheer silence. I watch the faces of my fellow congregants returning from reception of communion. They are all ages, all races, all economic strata, in various stages of physical vigor, and each one's unique beauty shines forth. Sometimes it seems to fill the space; other times it is a faint presence. I'm reminded of Albert Einstein, who said of God, "Subtle is the Lord." One thing I know: being with that particular community of believers, open to the Word and aware of the presence, leaves an imprint on me difficult to ignore. That alone is not enough, of course, to ensure courage in my daily living. But as a Catholic, I know that my community extends beyond the walls of my small church. It extends throughout the world, and I am enlightened and encouraged and strengthened by distant others, including Pope Benedict XVI, who chose, in his first encyclical, to write about God's love. "Love is the light—and in the end the only light—that can give us the courage needed to keep living and working" (*Deus Caritas Est*, No. 39). Being part of a worshipping community, local and universal, is like tending a garden in fertile times and times of drought. The fruitfulness comes from faithful tending.

Praying Alone

Dedicated gardeners know experientially that time apart, in solitude and silence, is also essential to nourish the inscape. In *7 Essentials for the Spiritual Journey* I wrote about a young woman, Margaret, who gardens in a large communal space but who goes there to get in touch with the deepest, most silent parts of her inner world. "When I go to the garden alone, I go to a different place in myself," she told me. "Because of this I can be more alone in the garden than anywhere else, even when there are other gardeners working nearby. And the silence of the garden is large, even while the normal sounds of life can be heard. I can experience this solitude and silence while I work in the garden because my mind empties and clears and time ceases to exist. If there is any heaviness in my life, it dissipates and I am lighter. In creating order in the garden there is order in my life. I work slowly without haste. I put seeds and seedlings in the ground. I water and weed and tend and wait. But the waiting isn't hard because it's the process of the garden that gives pleasure and peace" (56–57).

Margaret's experience of gardening is a true metaphor for the inner life of prayer. We know that we can't see the garden growing right away; it develops in the dark, slowly. In the words of Margaret, "we water and weed and tend and *wait*." So, too, with personal prayer. Waiting is a critical component. When we stop our frantic activity, we realize more consciously that, in fact, we are always waiting for God. Can there be better preparation for living in and through experiences of natural disasters? The miracle of the garden shines light on the miracles of the inscapes.

Praying the psalms in the solitary gardens of our souls is a "tending" kind of thing; the wisdom of waiting is in the songs of praise and passion. It's not as if the psalmist finds waiting easy, certainly not at first, and neither do we. But over time, wisdom sprouts and grows strong as we learn needed lessons. Then we can say truthfully, "I will sing praise to the Lord while I live." Praying in solitude is the other side of a worshipping community.

Cultivating the Mind

Jesuit theologian and philosopher Bernard Lonergan has given the world a helpful schema for navigating our interior terrains. His imperatives stress the need to *be attentive, be intelligent, be reasonable, be responsible, and be loving*. Worship and solitude can certainly help us to be more attentive to our experience and to the world in which we live. But that, of course, is not enough. Lonergan's next step is to be intelligent; that is, to gather data and then to explore the various implications of what we see and think we know—and to continue to gather data. To be intelligent is to respect what the mind is capable of knowing.

When my young son so many years ago told me about tornadoes and the unlikelihood of their making angular turns, I was so grateful that he had been paying attention and could bring some intelligence to our problem.

More recently, a ten-year-old British girl saved one hundred other tourists from the Asian tsunami by warning them that a giant mass of water was on its way. How did she know? She learned about the phenomenon weeks earlier at school. "I was on the beach and the water started to go funny," Tilly Smith told a newspaper, *The Sun*, in an interview from Thailand (reported by Reuters). "There were bubbles and the tide went out all of a sudden. I recognized what was happening and had a feeling there was going to be a tsunami. I told Mummy." Tilly recognized the danger signs because she had done a school project on giant waves caused by underwater earthquakes. Quick action by Tilly's mother and Thai hotel staff meant the beach was quickly cleared just minutes before a huge wave crashed ashore. No one was killed on that beach.

What's to be learned from these vignettes? Perhaps one thing is that children's knowledge, learned in an environment of simple factual information and conveyed non-ideologically, is an important and authentic means of communication. And perhaps it would benefit all of us to engage with like simplicity and openness to information.

Another thing to be learned is that believers can decide to go more deeply into the dialogue between science and religion, not only to be free from ideological confines, but in order to appreciate more deeply the grandeur of God. "Nature is never spent," writes the Jesuit poet Gerard Manley Hopkins in "God's Grandeur": "There lives the dearest freshness deep down things…"

Theologians like Polkinghorne or John Haught of Georgetown University invite us to ponder these deep down things, to move toward a reverence for God that goes beyond images, to the Mystery that pervades the universe. The result, for me, is a sense of One who abides with me (the Paraclete) yet is definitely *not* made in my image, and who offers me a life of discovery beyond all images, brooding "with warm breast and with ah! bright wings" (Hopkins, "God's Grandeur"). And there is also the opportunity to recognize and act upon my responsibility for preserving the planet in its grandeur.

About Landscapes and Inscapes:
Some Conclusions

Embedded in the stories and lore of natural disasters is the human inclination to reach out to God either through familiar prayer or through acts of compassion and solidarity. During Hurricane Carol, Mrs. Wholey threw a medal into the rising water; Rosaries were said as the situation worsened. These actions are in the well-established Catholic lineage of invoking Mary's assistance in time of danger.

Also embedded are the ancient questions surrounding God's will: Did God cause the disaster? Did humans cause it? How should we look upon chaos in our landscapes? After an earthquake in India refigured the natural landscape, the social landscape was reshaped with a new spirit of equality and community, a testimony to the capacity of the human spirit for renewal.

This essay has tried to hold the traditional ways of coping with the unexpected, in tension with new understandings about God and the created order. Being committed to a faith-community through communal prayer and shared values, and being committed to cultivating one's inner space through personal prayer, study, and works of mercy and justice, are tested and reliable ways of tending to the spirit.

11

But contemporary Christian theologians, as knowledgeable in the field of science as they are in biblical scholarship, are helping to bring into focus a way of thinking about God that goes beyond images and yet adds to the tradition. These new theologians employ not only science in their work, but linguistics and cultural anthropology as well. The result is an expanded horizon for exploring God as creator, and for seeing creation as dynamic and ongoing. Questions of grace and human cooperation with grace can be probed freely in such an open environment. This interdisciplinary approach encourages collaboration and is yielding the richest of dialogues.

Questions for Reflection

1. Do you agree with the statement that creation is ongoing and that what we term a "natural disaster" is often the result of the creative process?
2. Do you think that a committed Christian can draw on traditional spiritual practices and still be open to the discoveries of scientific research?
3. How do you get in touch with faith (i.e., trust in God) when faced with a situation out of your control?
4. To what extent do you recognize human responsibility in relation to natural disasters? For example, what changes can people enact to protect the environment?

Bibliography

Chathanatt, John, SJ. "Unshaken Faith." *Indian Express,* n.d.

Jones, Arthur, and Dolores Leckey. *Facing Fear with Faith*. Notre Dame, IN: Ave Maria Press, 2001.

Leckey, Dolores. *7 Essentials for the Spiritual Journey*. New York: Crossroad, 1998.

Lonergan, Bernard. *Method in Theology*. Toronto: University of Toronto Press, 1971.

Polkinghorne, John. *Science and the Trinity*. New Haven, CT: Yale University Press, 2004.

Wiesel, Elie. *Night,* rev. ed. New York: Hill and Wang, 2006.

What's God Got to Do with It?
Natural Disasters and Moral Agency
Kevin J. O'Neil, CSsR

The daily newspaper often brings stories of violence by one human being against another that leave us with our mouths agape, asking the question, "How could anyone do such a thing?" Weren't those words on our lips, in some form or another, on that fateful day in September of 2001? Don't we raise the question when we hear of the abuse of children, or of persons abandoned by those entrusted with their care? We cannot fathom doing such a thing ourselves and are dumbfounded as to how anyone else can. Underlying our question, of course, is a rather optimistic view: we are baffled and outraged by inhuman behavior. Thank God that we are still stunned at our inhumanity toward one another.

What is significant about asking "How could anyone do such a thing?" in the face of tragic news is that we can ordinarily point to a perpetrator of an act and question him or her about this atrocity. We want answers. Still stymied, we might look further into the person's background and character to find the roots of inhuman behavior.

Catholic moral tradition would recognize the wisdom in what we do. Traditionally, an act for which a person may be held responsible requires two conditions: the person who acts must freely choose to do so and must be aware of what he or she is doing. Freedom and knowledge, the tradition says, are requirements of a human act. In addition, one's culpability depends on the degree to which one's freedom and knowledge are unimpeded by such things as fear, ignorance, passion, and the like. For example, a woman who denounces her country while being held hostage has her freedom compromised and is not as responsible for her action as someone who deliberately chooses to do so. Similarly, a man who accidentally shoots a person, mistaking him for a deer or another animal, would not be held as morally responsible for his error, due to ignorance, as someone who intentionally shoots a person. In each of these cases, the person's culpability is not completely removed, but it is lessened because of fear or ignorance. The more free and aware people are, the more culpable they are for their actions.

In contrast to tragedy bought about by the free choice of human beings, natural disasters—like the horrific tsunami at Christmas of 2004 and hurricanes Katrina and Rita that battered the Gulf Coast of the United States in the summer of 2005—occur apart from human agency for the most part. There is no one to point to or to accuse. In these moments of overwhelming devastation, we do not ask, "How could anyone do that?" because we know that these events are not the result of human freedom and knowledge. Without the face of a specific human moral agent or perpetrator, persons of faith often ask, "How could God allow this to happen?" or even, "How could God do this?"

The theme of this book, looking for God in natural disasters, raises questions about responsibility for natural disasters. Is it the work of God and, if so, how could God do such a thing? If not the direct work of God, as I will argue, where is God to be found in natural disasters? Finally, if one is to attribute some moral responsibility for natural disasters, where might one look? In this brief essay I would like to begin to respond to some of these queries through the particular lens of the theological discipline of moral theology or Christian ethics.

What Image of God Is at Work in Our Questioning?

One of the first topics for consideration is the image of God that is at work in responses to natural disasters. Does God choose to send natural disasters as a form of punishment? Does God allow natural disasters to occur? Even if we say that God is not directly the cause, is he not ultimately the one responsible since this is God's world with God's plan?

I will focus my response first on the question as to whether God causes natural disasters. This image of God is false, I believe. It is inconsistent with the God revealed in Jesus Christ.

14

Kevin J. O'Neil, CSsR

Does God Cause Natural Disasters as a Punishment?

In reaction to natural disasters, some people state unabashedly that these events are God's responses to moral depravity. Calling to mind the God revealed particularly in the Old Testament, some would describe natural disasters as truly acts of God, acts freely chosen by God as a punishment for the sins of people.

Michael Marcavage, the director of the Christian fundamentalist organization Repent America, stated only two days after Hurricane Katrina struck:

> Although the loss of lives is deeply saddening, this act of God destroyed a wicked city.... New Orleans was a city that had its doors wide open to the public celebration of sin. From the devastation may a city full of righteousness emerge.... We must help and pray for those ravaged by this disaster, but let us not forget that the citizens of New Orleans tolerated and welcomed the wickedness in their city for so long.... May this act of God cause us all to think about what we tolerate in our city limits, and bring us trembling before the throne of Almighty God. (Repent America, 2005)

In a less developed argument, Mayor Ray Nagin of New Orleans said on January 16, 2006, "Surely God is mad at America. He sent us hurricane after hurricane after hurricane."

I find this image of God incompatible with the God revealed in Jesus Christ. I do not believe that God is capable, by nature, of choosing such destruction for his people. Immediate objections arise. What about the flood at the time of Noah? What about the plagues sent to the people of Egypt? What about countless battles won by God for the Israelites? All of these references are to the God of the Old Testament, a God not yet fully revealed in the person of his Son, Jesus Christ.

Yet, are there not texts from the New Testament, even "words" from Jesus himself, that would support a punishing God? Two particular passages of Matthew's Gospel come to mind.

In the parable of the unmerciful servant (Matt 18:21–35), a man who is forgiven a huge debt by his master has another servant imprisoned for failing to pay him (the unmerciful servant) a debt. When the other servants witness this injustice, they bring the unmerciful servant before the lord who throws him into prison. The parable concludes with words from Jesus: "So my heavenly Father will also do to every one of you, if you do not forgive your brother or sister from your heart."

A more frequently used and better known text is the parable of the sheep and the goats from Matthew 25. After addressing those who failed to feed the hungry or clothe the naked or visit those in prison, the king says, "You that are accursed, depart from me into the eternal fire prepared for the devil and his angels" (v. 41). He condemns them to the fires of hell for their lack of attention to "one of the least of these who are members of my family" (v. 40).

If God is capable of inflicting punishment on these individuals, the unforgiving servant and the inattentive selfish ones, can he not also inflict punishment through natural disasters on many people?

Leaving aside the fact that many innocent people suffer as a result of natural disasters, the response to the question is still no. Regarding the scriptures, we must remember that these stories are not always precise descriptions of how God acts but that they are to move listeners to a change of heart. But what can we say regarding God as the one who directly wills harm on people, the one who causes natural disasters?

Is God Capable of Causing Natural Disasters? Moral Character and Moral Action

My thesis is that God cannot will natural disasters; God cannot even will eternal condemnation for human beings. This does not mean that people cannot go to hell. But if they do, it is not God's doing, but their own. On what basis can I make these claims? Precisely on the revelation by Jesus of who God is. The most succinct description of God is "God is love" (1 John 4:8).

I began this essay by referring to an experience that I believe is common: seeing tragedy we ask, how could someone do such a thing? We are shocked at what harm a human being can do to another. Yet our experience tells us that, sadly, we are capable of great injustices and untold violence toward one another.

God is not capable of such evil. If, as we said, human beings require freedom and knowledge to perform a fully human act, so, by analogy, does God. But what does it mean for God to be free? More to the point, what is true freedom?

To be free is not, as we commonly think, to be able to make a choice. To be free is to be able to make a choice for what is good. We mistakenly think, and might say, "I am free to choose to be kind to you or to hurt you." But true freedom exists only when one chooses what is good. Any other choice is not really free but an example of our being slaves to the attraction of evil. Further, our choices arise from the type of people that we are; they are born of our moral character and shape us as persons. So, we expect honest people to be truthful, just people to be fair, and charitable people to be loving. We are often surprised by people who act "out of character." Their behavior catches us off guard because they act contrary to what our experience of them would have us expect. This inconsistency, evident, for example, when a person whom we consider generally honest lies to us, is the result of sin.

God is untainted by sin; God desires nothing but our good. When God exercises freedom, it can only be for our good. God cannot will natural disasters as a means of punishment, nor does God even condemn sinners to hell. It is not in God's nature to do so. And, unlike us, God cannot act "out of character." Whereas we, affected as we are by sin, are capable of abusing our freedom, God cannot do so. God will not do so. Perhaps some further reflection on God's relationship to punishment and even eternal condemnation could be helpful.

In a very concise catechesis on hell given in 1999, Pope John Paul II carefully described the Catholic tradition on hell and the distinct role that God plays and that we human beings play. God's goodness and mercy are without limits, said the pope. It is we human beings who can freely close ourselves off from God's love, mercy, and forgiveness, and consequently break our communion with God for all eternity. Critical for our reflections is the pope's description of God as one whose goodness and mercy are infinite. This statement is a reiteration of who God is and what we can expect of God.

What of eternal punishment, then? Is it not an act of God, something that God chooses for unrepentant sinners? It is not. The tragedy is that we human beings choose that as well. John Paul II, in the same cat-echesis, emphasized that hell is not a place but rather the state of people who cut themselves off completely and definitively from God. If someone ends up in hell, it is not because God wants hell for the person. God wants our salvation. Rather, we say no to God, the one who is love. To be damned, then, is to have one's relationship with God ruptured as a result of one's own free choice. If one dies in this state, one will be forever sep-arated from God. The judgment of God, then, is a ratification of the state, freely chosen, by the creature.

We must, then, reject an image of God that places natural disas-ters as free choices of God in order to punish sinners. We ought not to look to God as the moral agent taking vengeance on the just and the unjust alike.

Experiencing God's Presence

If God is not to be found as the moral agent who freely chooses to inflict punishment by means of natural disasters, where is God to be found in those tragic times? If we are looking for God in natural disasters, where might we see his face? I suggest, once again, that the answer lies in the rev-elation of Jesus Christ. God's action is to be found not in the destructive power of uncontrollable hurricanes, earthquakes, floods, and the like. Rather, God's action is found in his life-sustaining presence and in the response of people, a response born of their compassion and solidarity.

Although we attribute extraordinary moments in salvation his-tory to God's free and conscious action, God's ordinary way of acting in the world is through human beings like ourselves; he relied on judges, kings, prophets, and seers to communicate his message and to reach out to his people. The definitive moment, in this regard, is when the extraor-dinary met the ordinary: when divinity and humanity came together in the flesh and blood of Jesus of Nazareth—an event of cosmic signifi-cance, yet as common as the birth of a child.

How is God "acting," then? How is God's freedom being exer-cised? God has created the world and called all of life to come to its full-ness. Unique among creation is human life, made in God's image and likeness. Although God calls human beings to the fullness of life, we do not always respond to that invitation. Sometimes we act contrary to goodness and love, contrary to God's designs for us. Yet God is still acting, moving us by his Spirit and tugging at us to come to him, to come to truth, goodness, and love. But God does not force us to do so; God always invites and waits. There is no question, however, that his will for us is for our flourishing here on earth and our experiencing eternal happiness with him afterward.

Is it not possible that something similar occurs even in the natural world? Could it be that the natural world is also slowly evolving toward the fullness of life, the paradise imagined in the first chapter of Genesis, and that God responds to the natural world in the same way that he responds to us? In other words, just as human beings do not always do what God desires for us, yet God does not step in and punish us but leaves us free, is it not possible that, at times and for a variety of reasons, the natural world also "acts," and I use the word by analogy, in a way that is contrary to God's design? There are cataclysmic natural disasters that kill thousands and hundreds of thousands of people. Surely God does not want this, does not choose it, yet it occurs "on his watch," so to speak. What we often expect or hope is that God, who is all-loving and merciful, would step in and stop creation from bringing destruction. But God does not do so, any more than he steps in to hold back the arm of an assassin or to prevent a child from drowning, any more than he intervened to save his Son. God acts, to be sure, but in much more subtle and almost invisible ways. God's action occurs on at least two levels.

God acts as the source of life. Even in the midst of willful human harm and natural disasters, God continues to sustain the created world and to call it to the fullness of life. God is life who holds all life in existence. God's very presence is an action that keeps creation alive. It is also a personal presence. God is not passive; it is not as if he stands by idly and watches the developing world. Rather, much as *we* might stand *beside* someone we love, wanting their good and loving them in the midst of their joys and suffering, so too is God in the world. Yet, God's presence is even more. God is present within the victims themselves, closer to them than we could ever be. So, God's action is found in both his life-sustaining power and his loving presence. God doesn't step in and control the world, but stands in loving relationship with us in the midst of all that we experience, calling us, even in suffering and death, to life and love.

God is also present and acts in the compassionate response of human beings to one another. In his first encyclical, *God Is Love*, Pope

Benedict XVI articulates the various ways in which God is manifested to us. Among them, he simply notes that we encounter God through one another, through people that reflect God's presence to us (§17). More precisely, when human beings act out of goodness and love, it is *they* who are acting in God, who is really the source of all goodness and love. In a limited way they participate in the infinite goodness and love of God. It is not as if God acts and then human beings come along; or that human beings do some good and then God blesses it. The works of charity and justice that we perform as human beings flow from the creative power of God and witness to God's presence among us and within us. The outpouring of assistance to victims of natural disasters, whether viewed by volunteers as collaboration with God or not, is an instance of the justice and love and charity of God at work in the world.

I remember one time on a mission listening to a woman who told of three friends who, within weeks of one another, were all diagnosed with cancer; they were all young women, late thirties to early forties. She simply talked of the gentleness and care that they had for one another, and also her own guilt that she was the only healthy one. She told stories of these friends taking turns bringing meals to one another's families, accompanying each other to appointments with the doctor; just one charitable act after another. After telling these beautiful stories of care, she took me off guard when she began to cry as she asked me, "Where is God in all this? Where is God?" Aware of her own fragility at that moment, I simply asked her, "Couldn't God be right there in the midst of all four of you? Taking one another to the doctor? Preparing meals? Babysitting? Simply sitting with one another?" "I never thought of God that way," she said. "But it makes sense."

Doesn't it make sense that a God who chose to take on our flesh to redeem the world would continue to sit with people in their suffering and to call people to the fullness of life through flesh and blood like us, through the presence of this woman and her friends, through their compassionate concern for one another?

Looking for God in natural disasters may mean that we rethink the God whom we are looking for and the way he will act. In a recent visit to the concentration camp at Auschwitz, Pope Benedict XVI—acknowledging that the atrocities carried out in the camps prompted the question "Where is God?"—observed that our crying out to God ought to be a cry to one another as well, a cry that touches our hearts, where

God resides. We appeal not to a distant "out there" God but to the God who wants to work through us, but whose power is often stifled by self-absorption, apathy, or opportunism. Although our tradition speaks of God as omnipotent, omniscient, and omnipresent, the God revealed in Jesus enters our world as a vulnerable child and invites the world to receive him. God continues to act in the world through us. At times our cries to God for help are also cries to one another, to the best of our humanity, for comfort and love.

Ultimately, we ought not to look for God as the cause of natural disasters but, rather, seek him in the responses of people to the suffering of one another. There, God is to be found. There, God continues to effect his will for the flourishing of creation even in the midst of tragedy and devastation.

Is Anyone Responsible for Natural Disasters?

What of moral culpability for natural disasters, then? Can we point to anyone as the cause or the one somehow implicated in disasters? Not as easily, it would seem, as in the uncomplicated case where moral agents freely choose to abuse their freedom and harm others.

Perhaps, however, there is a link between human behavior and natural disasters that is not so immediately evident. The connection is sometimes on a cosmic scale and other times is very specific to the location of the disaster. Using the United States' experience of hurricanes Katrina and Rita in the summer of 2005, I would like to suggest a possible correlation between human agency and natural disasters.

On the cosmic level, some scientists argue for a connection between lack of care for the environment, resulting in particular in global warming and the occurrence of natural disasters. They suggest that the rising temperature of ocean waters contributes to the strength that hurricanes will have in the future (National Oceanic and Atmospheric Administration). There is clearly no unanimity on this point, but even the slightest evidence of damage to the environment due to the release of greenhouse gases warrants careful reflection on the part of the human family, who are called to be good stewards of creation. The Catholic bishops of the United States, in their 2001 statement on global climate change, remind us that authentic stewardship will demand changes both in our behavior and in the way in which we advance technically. Failure to make these changes would clearly raise questions about the abuse of freedom that will impact future generations.

Pope John Paul II raised significant questions in this regard. In a 1996 address on the environment he noted that we are dealing with both ethical and ecological issues and asked how to ensure that fast-paced development does not ultimately turn against humanity, the very ones it is to serve. The question is about preventing future devastation of our world but also about dealing with harm to the environment that has already occurred.

News reports in the wake of the devastating Hurricane Katrina carried stories of a lack of preparation for a hurricane of that magnitude and a sluggish response to her victims. Other articles stated that there was no adequate evacuation plan for the residents of the city, and that many people might have been spared death or injury if there had been better planning for, and implementation of, an evacuation of the city. Many people suggested that racism was at work because the hurricane affected primarily not the wealthy but mostly the poor African American residents of the Gulf Coast. Other reports said that the Army corps of engineers had not built adequate levies to contain the waters; thus the city of New Orleans seemingly suffered more damage from the breach of the levies meant to keep water out of the city than from the hurricane winds themselves.

Although it is possible that some of these situations were the result of the action of one person or the combined apathy of many, it is more likely a systemic lack of attention to matters that should have been taken care of. The Catholic moral tradition speaks of social sin, which is a way to address the structures or systems that oppress people when it is difficult to point to a specific sinner or person responsible for the evil. A social sin, like racism, for example, is part of the air that we breathe. While we may be able to point to individuals who are racist, the social sin of racism is larger than any one individual and has the potential of offending the dignity, or harming the well-being, of countless persons. There is little doubt that social sin contributed to the devastation of the hurricanes of 2005 in the United States.

There is no question that the hurricanes vastly damaged the Gulf Coast. It was, however, the reality of social sin, perhaps apathy or even sloth on the part of many, that compounded the tragedy. As Pope John

Paul II pointed out in his encyclical *On the Hundredth Anniversary of Rerum Novarum*, these structures of sin must be addressed if reconstruction is to be successful and future destruction is to be avoided. These structures of sin, this systemic affront to the dignity of persons, did not arise overnight, nor will they necessarily be dismantled with speed. Doing so requires patience and courage, but it is a task that must be done so that human beings may live in community in such a way as to flourish (*Centesimus annus* §38).

If we attempt to locate some moral responsibility and culpability for natural disasters, we might look at our tolerance of sinful structures. Evil, the absence of God and good, is present in systems that oppress people and foster a lack of genuine concern for them, especially the poor and the underprivileged. On the other hand, God and goodness are to be found in the compassionate, loving presence of people and their action for justice.

Conclusion

In chapter nine of John's Gospel, the disciples ask Jesus about the cause of a man's blindness: "Rabbi, who sinned, this man or his parents, that he was born blind?" (v. 2). The disciples look for the cause of the evil in the man's life. But Jesus directs their attention not to the cause of the blindness but how it might serve God's designs now. "Neither this man nor his parents sinned; he was born blind so that God's works might be revealed in him. We must work the works of him who sent me while it is day," replies Jesus (vv. 3–4a).

There is no doubt that, in the face of natural disasters and untold human suffering and devastation, we would like to make sense of it and often attempt to do so by questions: "Why did this happen? Where is God in all of this? Why did God let this happen?" Yet, perhaps the better questions are these: "What are we to do now? How can we respond to tragedy so as to use it for God's will for his people and this world?"

To imitate God in these circumstances would consist in being present to and in solidarity with victims in their suffering. Just as Jesus cured the blind man in John's Gospel, we too should "work the works" of God by opening ourselves to his call to compassion, justice, and charity toward our brothers and sisters.

Both the wonders and tragedies of life remind us that we stand before something much greater than ourselves. Theologian Robert Barron has described our experience of looking at the world as like having our noses up against the canvas of a painting. It is impossible for us to see the whole picture. In the face of our own limitations and the mystery of God, we might make our own the following prayer by Kevin Axe. By doing so we may both find the face of God in natural disasters and manifest God's presence to others.

> May God bless you with discomfort at easy answers, half truths, and superficial relationships, so that you may live deep within your heart. And may God bless you with tears to shed for those who suffer from pain, rejection, starvation, and war, so that you may reach out your hand to comfort them and to turn their pain into joy. ("When Bad Weather Happens to Good People," 33)

Questions for Reflection

1. What do I think God is doing when natural disasters occur? How does my response square with what I believe about God? Does it?
2. What is *my* question? Where is God? Why does God do or allow this? Why doesn't God stop it? What do *I* ask?
3. What experience of God have I had in the "natural disasters" of my life, for example, hurricane, sickness, death, loss, and the like? Did I feel God's presence? What was I expecting of God?
4. How might I raise my own consciousness of social sin and of ways in which I might tolerate or even promote it by the way that I think, speak, or act?
5. Can I recall a moment from my own life where I either experienced God's compassionate presence in another or when I was God's face to someone in his or her suffering?

References

Axe, Kevin. "When Bad Weather Happens to Good People." *U.S. Catholic*, 66/1 (January 2001): 30–33.

Benedict XVI. *God Is Love*. Encyclical letter. December 25, 2005. Found at http://www.vatican.va/holy_father/benedict_xvi/encyclicals/documents/hf_ben-xvi_enc_20051225_deus-caritas-est_en.html (last accessed May 30, 2006).

———. "Visit to the Auschwitz Camp." May 28, 2006. Found at http://www.vatican.va/holy_father/benedict_xvi/speeches/2006/may/documents/hf_ben-xvi_spe_20060528_auschwitz-birkenau_en.html (last accessed May 30, 2006).

John Paul II. "International Solidarity Needed to Safeguard Environment." Address by the Holy Father to the European Bureau for the Environment. *L'Osservatore Romano* (June 26, 1996). Quoted in USCCB, *Global Climate Change*. Washington, DC: United States Conference of Catholic Bishops, 2001.

———. *On the Hundredth Anniversary of Rerum Novarum*. Encyclical letter. May 1, 1991. Found at http://www.vatican.va/edocs/ENG0214/_INDEX.HTM.

———. Wednesday audience, July 28, 1999. Found at http://www.vatican.va/holy_father/john_paul_ii/audiences/1999/documents/hf_jp-ii_aud_28071999_en.html (last accessed May 29, 2006).

Johnson, Elizabeth. "Does God Play Dice? Divine Providence and Chance." *Theological Studies* 57 (1996): 3–18.

National Oceanic and Atmospheric Administration. Geophysical Fluid Dynamics Laboratory. "Global Warming and Hurricanes." Found at http://www.gfdl.noaa.gov/~tk/glob_warm_hurr.html.

Repent America. "Hurricane Katrina Destroys New Orleans Days before 'Southern Decadence.'" Press Release. August 31, 2005. Found at http://www.repentamerica.com/ pr_hurricanekatrina.html (last accessed May 18, 2006).

United States Conference of Catholic Bishops. *Global Climate Change: A Plea for Dialogue, Prudence, and the Common Good*. Washington, DC: United States Conference of Catholic Bishops, 2001. Found at http://www.usccb.org/sdwp/international/globalclimate.htm (last accessed May 30, 2006).

3

Out of the Depths I Cry to You, O LORD

Dianne Bergant, CSA

During December of 2004, I was in India giving lectures to a group of religious leaders. I had been in the north of the country on the twenty-sixth of that month when the tsunami swept across the Indian Ocean, destroying everything in its path. The country was understandably traumatized by this tragedy, terrified people not knowing where to go, what to do, or whom to reach. Several individuals who had registered for the conference at which I was to speak canceled, rightly believing that their place was with their people. As is often the case with such a gathering of religious leaders, we opened those mornings with the celebration of the Eucharist, though for most of us, the idea of celebration was furthest from our minds. Rather, we gathered to commemorate the death and resurrection of Jesus as we mourned the tragic deaths of so many and prayed for their resurrection.

As a biblical theologian, I am particularly sensitive to the manner in which the message of the Lectionary readings of the day is preached. On December 30, the day of my presentations, I had nothing to worry about in this regard, for the homilist never even referred to the readings. However, I was unprepared for what he did say. While the scope of this natural disaster was still unfolding before our eyes, and to a group of religious leaders of the country, many of whom had suffered personal loss, the homilist described the catastrophe that was enveloping thousands of people as the just retribution of an avenging God. (I discovered later that he was not the only preacher who proclaimed that same message.)

In my view, the circumstances surrounding the tsunami called for a message of consolation and trust in the loving providence of God, rather than one of judgment. Still, I cannot deny the fact that our religious tradition, particularly our biblical tradition, is replete with references to some aspect of the theme of retribution—righteousness is rewarded and wickedness is punished. We find this theology in both biblical testaments. Furthermore, various forms of natural disaster are often depicted in the Bible as divine retribution. This prompts us to ask, Is there a relationship between the moral order in human life and the natural order of the world? Are natural disasters really punishment for human sin? In order to answer these questions, if only briefly, I would like to examine a few biblical passages that describe natural disasters; namely, the flood (Gen 6–8), the plagues, and the final destruction at the end of time.

Two Very Different Worldviews

There is no question that the ancient Israelites believed that their God controls the forces of nature. This idea probably had originated much earlier in the ancient Near East, when the heavenly bodies such as the sun, moon, and stars were revered as independent deities. At that time, the forces of nature, especially forms of water such as rain and snow, were considered minor deities, daughters or sons of the major gods. Religious devotees sought to please these gods since the powers of nature that they controlled were essential for human life. People viewed the "blessings" of nature as signs that the gods were pleased, while the ravages of nature were evidence of the gods' displeasure. As the Israelites developed their unique monotheistic perspective, they appropriated to their one God the characteristics and powers formerly enjoyed by the entire pantheon of gods.

One principal difference between the perception of the cosmic rule of the earlier gods and that of the God of Israel was the basis of this new divine rule. God's cosmic rule was rooted not in brute power but in *tsᵉdāqāh*, the Hebrew word for righteousness. The verbal root of this word means "to be straight," or "to conform to the norm." In the tradition of ancient Israel, this norm was the nature and will of God. In reality, it is God who is righteous (Ps 145:17). Human beings are righteous only to the extent that they conform to God's will. Furthermore, righteousness and judgment, or justice *(mishpāt)*, were thought to be the foundation of God's throne (Ps 97:2). According to a prevailing ancient

Near Eastern creation tradition, the cosmic throne was set up only after order had been established.

Israel maintained that the same principle of righteousness governs the order on earth because the same Creator established all order in the beginning. They believed that what happens on one plane of reality has repercussions on another; disruption in one dimension of God's created order affects the harmony of the entire system. Such a worldview held that moral order and natural order are inherently interrelated. This understanding of the structure of the world could easily hold that there may very well be a connection between wickedness and natural disaster.

The covenant theology found in the Hebrew Scriptures reflects this relationship between morality and the rest of creation, and it builds on it. Israel believed that its law made specific the moral order established at creation, the moral order that was to be observed. The rewards and sanctions associated with its law drew clear lines connecting morality and the natural order. It follows from this that when women and men live lives of integrity, submissive to the orders of the universe, the balance within creation will be maintained and all creatures will enjoy peace and ecological tranquility. Correlatively, sin upsets that delicate balance established by God at creation, and the consequences of the imbalance will be felt in natural disasters such as flood, drought, or infertility of any kind. Because of the structure of this multilayered order, fidelity to God ensures the people's prosperity in the land, while faithlessness puts into motion a series of events that can wreak havoc on the whole earth. The flood narrative in the Book of Genesis should be understood with this worldview as background.

This ancient Near Eastern worldview may appear quite naïve to contemporary believers, whose perception of order in the natural world rests on sophisticated scientific understanding. We perceive the natural world in a way very different from that of our religious ancestors. We may acknowledge that human actions do have repercussions on the rest of creation, but this is because of the fundamental interdependence among the various dimensions of natural creation, not because God uses the natural world as an agent of reward and/or punishment.

It is true that in some situations people must accept a degree of responsibility for some of the natural misfortunes that they suffer. For example, floods can devastate property and threaten lives when people disregard the natural contour of the land and build on floodplains or simple landfills. Flooding can also occur when trees which normally drink heavily of available water and whose roots hold the soil in place, are cut down indiscriminately and not replaced. So much of the ecological devastation from which we suffer today is the direct result of unbridled greed and of disdain for what cannot immediately satisfy human needs or desires. These attitudes are both sinful and foolish. We, like every other creature of the natural world, are embedded in the reality of this world; we are not above it. Furthermore, like every other creature of the natural world, we are subject to its laws, laws established in the beginning by the Creator. In many ways we have experienced what the ancients professed: that those who live in accord with the laws of nature are blessed by the very creation that they respect, and those who violate such laws often experience nature's revenge. The natural world works synergistically, and if we are to survive within it, we must abide by its laws and not expect it to live according to ours.

What, then, are we to think of the biblical passages that describe natural disasters as God's punishment for our sin? These passages demonstrate that our religious ancestors struggled with the same question that confounds us today: Why has this catastrophe happened to us? Their understanding of the integrated structure of the natural world provided them with an answer: Our moral failure has upset the delicate balance of the universe. Though we are faced with the same question, our scientific grasp of the forces of nature prevents us from proposing the answer in the same way. Our failure to understand and respect the interdependent character of natural creation is indeed the cause of some environmental calamities. However, such situations occur because the laws of nature have been violated, not social or cultic laws. Today we look for natural causes when *we* pose the question of why this catastrophe has happened to us.

As important as scientific explanation is, it does not help us understand biblical passages that describe natural disaster as punishment for sin. Ecological responsibility notwithstanding, we might not conclude, as our religious ancestors did, that the cause of the disaster is to be placed at the door of human error. However, we are in agreement with them that God certainly plays a role in the matter. And so we might be prompted to revise the original question and, when a natural disaster strikes, ask instead: Why has *God* done this to us? While the ancients would have been able to turn again to their concept of a multilayered universe for an answer, modern women and men whose worldview is more scientific cannot. Such a worldview forces us to revise, not only our understanding of the universe, but our perception of God as well.

Despite the revolutionary shift that scientific discovery has produced in our understanding, the biblical story of the flood continues to provide religious meaning for us today. Behind the story itself, there may very well have been an actual horrendous flood that devastated the land and swallowed up a large segment of the population. The vulnerability of the people was no match for the force of the turbulent water. Believing that the water itself was a manifestation of divine power, the people credited the flood to the action of God. Convinced that God was righteous and not capricious, they looked to the character of their lives for a reason for God's wrath. Such a story would have served as a warning for succeeding generations, exhorting them to fidelity lest a similar or worse fate befall them. Despite the differences between ancient and contemporary perception and worldview, the story reminds us today that we might have discovered some of the powers of nature, but we cannot really control them. While the biblical story does not explain why there are natural disasters, it does remind us that the forces of nature are in God's hands.

Signs and Wonders

The account of the ten plagues (Exod 7–11) is well known to most people. The ancient Israelites considered them "signs and wonders," manifestations of divine power that worked to Israel's benefit. The Egyptians, on the other hand, must certainly have seen them as plagues, afflictions that wrought havoc in the land. The account describes the pollution of the Nile River and all other Egyptian water supplies, infestations of frogs, gnats, and flies, the onslaughts of pestilence and boils, hail and thunder, an overshadowing of locusts and darkness, and finally, the death of the firstborn.

Demythologizing tendencies that marked the early part of twentieth-century biblical scholarship considered this account a series of descriptions of very natural phenomena, the kind of phenomena that frequently occurred in that area of the world during a particular time of the year. Some have even argued that one natural infestation or phenomenon actually causes the next. Regardless of the degree of scientific or historical accuracy of such an interpretation, one must still explain both the reason for the biblical version and the nature of its theological meaning, for the story clearly states that those phenomena, scientifically understandable or not, were the direct result of divine intervention.

One interpretation maintains that the biblical account was part of a cult legend. This position is based on the stated reason why the Israelites demanded their release. There we read that God wanted the Israelites to be freed in order to worship in the desert. This demand was made to Pharaoh again and again (Exod 5:1; 7:16, 26; 8:16, 23; 9:1, 13; 10:3). Furthermore, the final "plague" included part of an ancient blood ritual, which was historicized and became part of the Passover celebration (Exod 12). One might conclude from this interpretation that the plagues describing natural phenomena were arranged in such a way as to suggest increasing severity.

Each affliction afforded the Egyptians an opportunity to repent. Failing this, another affliction ensued, and another, until the final adversity, the death of the firstborn. Whether or not this ritual theory is accepted, most interpreters agree that the central theme behind the tradition of the plagues is the manifestation of the sovereign power of YHWH, the God of Israel. This is clearly demonstrated in the biblical story itself. There we see that it is God who sends each individual plague. Then, after the plague is removed, it is God who hardens Pharaoh's heart so that he really cannot respond positively to Moses' request for release.

The sovereign power of God is not an insignificant theme. It is presumed throughout the entire Bible. In fact, all of the nations of the ancient Near Eastern world believed that their god(s) or goddess(es) exercised power over them, as well as over all of the circumstances of their lives and their environments. However, these were usually patron deities, whose exercise of power was normally territorially circumscribed. To move outside of the boundaries of one's tribe, or city-state, or nation was to remove oneself from the protection of one's own god and to place oneself in some way under the control of other deities. In other words, the God of Israel reigned in Israel, while Egypt was the realm of the Egyptian gods. To maintain that YHWH was able to wield power outside of the land of Israel was to make an extraordinary religious claim. It meant that the God of Israel was not limited by national boundaries.

The account of the plagues is not merely the report of a contest between Moses and Aaron and the magicians of Egypt, each side demonstrating its magical skills. This was a battle between the Pharaoh, who was believed to be in some way divine, and the God of Israel. It was a battle between deities. In a very real sense, it was a contest for the loyalties of the Israelite people. Which deity was stronger and, as a result, would win their allegiance? Though YHWH was already worshipped as the God of Israel's ancestors (Exod 2:23), the extent of God's saving power had not yet been revealed to them. In fact, the oppressive experience of the people in the land of Egypt suggested that their God was either powerless in another land or disinterested in the Israelites' affliction. The latter explanation is clearly not the case, for we read earlier in the text:

> Then the LORD said, "I have observed the misery of my people who are in Egypt; I have heard their cry on account of their taskmasters. Indeed, I know their sufferings, and I have come down to deliver them from the Egyptians, and to bring them up out of that land to a good and broad land, a land flowing with milk and honey." (Exod 3:7–8)

The account of the plagues shows that the first explanation is incorrect as well. In other words, God does indeed have both the power and the will to release the people from Egyptian bondage.

In the confrontation between Pharaoh and the God of Israel, the sides appear to have been equally matched, at least in the beginning. The Egyptian magicians were able to perform wondrous deeds that were comparable to those of Moses and Aaron (7:22, 8:3). This does not mean that YHWH was no more powerful than Pharaoh. Rather, it seems to have been a preliminary manifestation of divine power that rivaled that of the reigning sovereign. Even if God's power did not surpass that of Pharaoh, this would have been seen as remarkable, for the power of the God of Israel was thus seen as effective outside of the confines of the land of Israel. After the third plague, however, even the Egyptian wonder workers acknowledged the superior power of YHWH: "And the magicians said to Pharaoh, 'This is the finger of God!'" (8:19).

The biblical story does not suggest that God's initial plan was to defeat Pharaoh. Rather, it seems that God was asking simply that the people be allowed to go into the wilderness in order to worship their own God. It was because of Pharaoh's refusal to concede to this request that God's mighty power was manifested. The series of natural calamities was probably not meant to be a punishment for Pharaoh's obstinacy, but rather a demonstration of God's power over nature. Again and again, through the agency of Moses and Aaron, the scope of God's might was revealed. It was shown to be superior to that of the deities of the land, and it was exercised through the orders of nature. God commanded the waters and the animals of the earth, as well as the hail and darkness of the sky. Finally, in the death of the firstborn, the most terrifying event of all, God exercised control over life itself.

In reading the account of the plagues, we must remember that the worldview of the people among whom the tradition originated was quite different from ours today. As already seen in the examination of the flood narrative, the early Israelites believed that the same rules of order operated within the physical world as governed the moral world of human beings. Though the account of the plagues originated from within the same ancient worldview, this story functions in a slightly different way and with a significantly different purpose. In the earlier flood narrative, there is no question regarding the universal sovereignty of the God of Israel. That God has undisputed rule over the forces of nature. But here, universal sovereignty is the very point of the story. It might be called a confrontation story in which competing divine claims are put to the test.

Unlike the flood narrative that deals with cosmic forces, this story recounts natural phenomena occurring in the animal world. As already stated, such infestations may well have occurred in Egypt. However, the biblical writer takes the occasion to make several salient theological points. Chief among them is the universal sovereignty of the God of Israel. Not only was this God able to exercise power in the land of Pharaoh, but that power was also far superior to that of the Egyptians. Furthermore, since the Egyptians engaged in theriomorphic (animal-form) worship, the dominance of the God of Israel over animals would have been an insult to the very character of Egyptian worship.

What value might the account of the plagues have for contemporary believers? Even with the differences between the worldview of the past and that of the present, the theological force of the account remains the same; it acclaims the universal sovereignty of our God. One might think that this theme has little to say to professed monotheists who might not ever envision paying homage to another deity. However, they should not be too quick to draw this conclusion about themselves. There have always been forces in life and in the world that challenge our total commitment to God. Today they might not take the form of animals, but of economic prosperity, security, social dominance, military prowess, or scientific control. This account should remind us that nothing in the world can rival the sovereignty of God. It can also serve as a warning that these very aspects of the world to which we are inclined to give our allegiance might some day turn on us, and we could become their victims rather than their devotees.

The Great Tribulation

Within the recent past we have witnessed an upsurge of evangelical Christianity. The *Left Behind* series of books and movies has been a commercial success; the phenomenal draw of a new generation of preachers has given rise to the megachurch; and this religious perspective has demonstrated its influence in politics. Evangelicalism, vast and diverse as it may be, includes a variety of denominations of conservative Christian groups that emphasize a personal experience of conversion, the conviction that cultural issues should be grounded in Christian principles, and a biblically oriented faith. One tenet of that faith—namely, belief in the "great tribulation"—concerns us here.

Several passages from the New Testament mention a time of great suffering that will occur just before the Second Coming of Christ. This suffering received its name from a verse in the Gospel of Matthew:

> …for at that time there will be great tribulation, such as
> has not been since the beginning of the world until now,
> nor ever will be. (Matt 24:21, NAB)

The Gospel continues:

> Immediately after the tribulation of those days,
> the sun will be darkened,
>   and the moon will not give its light,
> and the stars will fall from the sky,
>   and the powers of the heavens will be shaken.
>   (Matt 24:29, NAB)

Visions found in the Book of Revelation augment the picture of this destruction. In that mysterious book, we read that the seventh seal is broken and angels blow trumpets that herald destruction in the heavens and on earth (Rev 7:12). Evangelical Christians interpret aspects of this "great tribulation" in various ways. Some maintain that Christians alive at that time will be taken bodily up into heaven (the rapture) before the actual suffering begins. Others believe that even Christians will have to taste the suffering before they are raptured into heaven. Still others hold that Christians will have to endure the suffering until Christ returns at the end of the tribulation.

From the very beginning, believers have wondered when these events might take place:

> But about that day and hour no one knows, neither the angels of heaven, nor the Son, but only the Father. For as the days of Noah were, so will be the coming of the Son of Man. (Matt 24:36–37)

The reference to the story of Noah is meant primarily to underscore the unexpectedness of the impending catastrophe. However, that reference also carries the connotation of natural disaster. Just what were the New Testament writers expecting? And how are we to understand such passages today?

Descriptions of this period of tribulation before the end-time belong to that aspect of Judeo-Christian faith known as eschatology, from the Greek word for "last things." Though this tradition included graphic accounts of appalling anguish and destruction, both physical and ecological, ancient Israel did not really believe that such calamity actually foreshadowed the end of the physical world. Rather, they thought that the suffering would be a purification of the world in preparation for a new and transformed era of peace and fulfillment. The distress was known as the "birthpangs of the messiah," the unavoidable suffering that accompanied the dawning of a new age.

Descriptions of tribulation that are both terrestrial and cosmic are characteristic of apocalyptic literature, such as is found in parts of Daniel (7–9) and Isaiah (24–27). Apocalyptic literature usually appeared at times of great anguish and unrest. It portrayed the world in a dualistic manner, illustrating how the struggle in which people found themselves was not merely a historical one, between social or political forces; it was also a cosmic struggle, including cosmic realms and heavenly beings. As pessimistic as this form of literature appears to be, it is really quite optimistic. Though the anguish described and actually endured may have been overwhelming, in the apocalyptic genre the forces of good always triumph over the forces of evil. Such an outcome would have been very consoling to those facing any form of suffering. It was meant to help them perceive how their personal misery might be a means of purifying themselves for participation in the age of fulfillment. Furthermore, the people were led to believe that their own suffering contributed to the final victory of righteousness.

This is the worldview behind the New Testament's references to the destruction of Jerusalem, which devout Jews would have considered the end of the age as they knew it (Matt 24:15–44, Mark 13, Luke 21:5–36). It also explains the apocalyptic character of the Book of Revelation, which reflects the struggles of the early Christians under the reign of the emperor Domitian. Apocalyptic teaching was always meant to encourage suffering people to remain faithful in their religious commitment because, regardless of how hopeless circumstances might appear, the forces of good would ultimately prevail. Furthermore, the anguish that they endured was really the birthpangs of the new age struggling to be born.

Today many people, both those who are evangelical and those who are not, read apocalyptic literature as if it were a prophetic portrayal of the contemporary world. They identify current political leaders in the guise of the beasts that terrorize the communities in those biblical accounts. They perceive natural disasters as the harbingers of the end of the world, which they believe is imminent. Because they interpret such calamities as God's way of purification in anticipation of the end, some are convinced that nothing can be done to prevent these disasters. Besides, depending upon how one understands the "great tribulation," they maintain that, through the rapture, the truly faithful will be preserved from torment.

Such an understanding is really a misunderstanding. Biblical apocalyptic literature, in both the Old and the New Testaments, was meant to be, not a prophecy of the end of the world, but a promise of the eventual end of the evil that seemed to have the upper hand. Despite its terrifying features, apocalyptic literature was not a message of doom and destruction, but one of hope and new life. Christians may have moved the locus of the fulfillment of that hope from this world to a world after death, but the primary focus of apocalyptic literature is the end of evil, not the end of the physical world.

How are *we* to read apocalyptic literature? If it does not foretell the destruction of the natural world, what meaning might it have for us today? The apocalyptic genre probably functions today as it did in the past. Rather than simply describe how bad circumstances can get, it assures us that regardless of how bad it gets, good will ultimately prevail. This message should encourage us, as it did our religious ancestors, to remain faithful regardless of the cost and to place our trust in God.

And So...

This essay was meant to demonstrate that natural disasters are not punishment from God for our sinfulness, or contests to demonstrate that our God is universally sovereign, or portents of the end of the world. Then how are believers to understand why God sends natural disasters, or allows them to happen? In order to answer such questions, we must return to the conclusions drawn above. First, we have come to realize that the natural world itself seemed to operate synergistically, holding everything in balance, though sometimes this balance may be at the expense of some aspect of the whole. In other words, what we consider a natural disaster may be nature readjusting itself, not God afflicting us.

Such an answer still does not explain why God does not protect us from the destructive forces of nature. This raises the theological question of theodicy, or the justice of God; why does a just God allow innocent people to suffer? This perennial question is addressed in the Book of Job: addressed, but never really answered. Though the reader knew that a wager had been agreed upon, Job was never told. Yet, when confronted with the splendor of the natural world, and through that world the magnificence of the Creator, Job withdrew his question (Why?) and placed himself in the hands of that Creator. If we believe that our God is universally sovereign, can we do less?

Yet, how are we to deal with the natural disasters when *we* fall victim to their power? Caught in the throes of terror and affliction, we might learn from those who found comfort in the apocalyptic literature.

They were not saved from their suffering, but they believed that if they remained faithful and trusted in God, ultimately they would not be lost. They believed that their suffering had the power to bring a new reality into being.

And so…, our biblical tradition may not answer the "Why did this happen?" of natural disasters, but it does offer us examples of "How are we to deal with it?" Subject to the laws of nature, we can only place ourselves in the hands of the God who fashioned those laws, confident that God wants what is best for us far more than we ourselves can imagine.

Questions for Reflection

1. How does our biblical faith help us to live with our human vulnerability in the face of natural disaster?
2. How can the forces of nature tell us about God?
3. How does biblical apocalyptic literature convey a message of hope?

4

God Is Watching Us— From a Distance

Francis J. Moloney, SDB

In the summer of 2004–2005 I was in an Australian beach town named Lorne. Born an Australian, I have spent many years in other parts of the world. For seven years I was a professor of New Testament at the Catholic University of America in Washington, DC. Each of those years, I managed to steal away in the middle of the northern winter to enjoy serving the Catholic parish of Our Lady of Fatima in the small town of Lorne. Along with family and friends, I experienced a January summer! The country town is generally quiet, well equipped for holiday makers and for business conventions all year round. The Catholic community at Lorne, served by a hard-working priest who covers no less than four parishes up and down the coastline that we know as "the Great Ocean Road," comprises about seventy families. It grows to two thousand in December to January each year. The people need, especially then, a full-time priest, and I have been happy to come from Washington, DC, to Lorne, Victoria, Australia, to sacrifice myself in their service!

Why tell this story? Because it was within that context that we watched, over and over again, the horror of the tsunami that hit the many coastlands just north of us, where thousands of Australians spend their holidays. Day after day we saw the list of dead and missing grow longer and longer. We cringed at the sight of the destruction the tsunami had left behind, the mass graves, the weeping parents and families, spouses and children, and we wondered why such things happen. We watched as others like us were lost forever in what was—at that time—probably the most televised natural disaster the world had followed. Even secular Australia allowed the theological question to emerge. In a country where religion is an intensely private matter, the newspapers and the chat rooms continually raised the question: Where was God in all of this? If God made the world (Gen 1:1–2:4a); fashioned it in, through, and for his Word, Jesus Christ (John 1:1–18, esp. vv. 3, 10); and holds creation in the palm of his hand (see, for example, Isa 40:26, 45:12, 48:13; John 5:17)—is this something God *wills?* If not, how could God let this happen? What sort of God lies behind such destruction and suffering?

Other disasters have happened since then that make this question even more urgent: the earthquake in Pakistan (quickly forgotten, but still a scar on the face of the earth), Hurricane Katrina (another TV blockbuster, made worse by subsequent human inefficiency and ill will), drought and death by starvation in the Sudan and other places in Africa (only occasionally drawn to our attention, as we have become somewhat deadened to this suffering). Even as I write these words, northern Australia is only beginning its recovery from the devastation of Cyclone Larry that hit the Queensland town of Innisfail. These are the spectacular examples of natural disaster that capture the public attention. They are rapidly and graphically delivered to us in our living rooms. But each individual and each family have their own inexplicable disasters to face, from the experience of the cot-death of a beloved child to the death by drowning of a young husband or wife at a beach picnic.

Communities and individuals of all and any religious persuasion are forced to ask the question I raised above: Where is God in this? If God can (and must) be traced somewhere in the midst of these tragedies, what sort of God can that be? What follows is an attempt to reflect upon, not resolve, that question from the perspective of a Christian biblical scholar. The themes of sin, evil, grace, and blessing lie at the heart of the biblical record, from its first pages to its last. These central biblical and theological themes depend upon the notion of God as the creator, and what is found in Genesis 1–3 is the bedrock of all subsequent biblical reference to creation. In the first section I will reflect upon these foundational biblical passages from the Hebrew Bible that deal with God the creator, Genesis 1–3. In the second section I will reflect further upon some fundamental Christian biblical texts from the Gospel of John and the Letters of Paul. No doubt more could be said, as there are other biblical reflections on God as creator, although all depend upon Genesis 1–3. Many such reflections deal with the tragedies and disasters that mark the human story. For the Bible, most of these but not all, are closely associated with human sinfulness. In the third section, on the basis of a limited

---

Francis J. Moloney, SDB

number of major biblical texts, I put forth a proposition that neither blames God nor eliminates God from natural disasters. And in conclusion, I suggest that perhaps we are not asking the right questions.

In my opinion, singer Bette Midler has it right: "God is watching us—from a distance." God's watching continues his loving attention to the mysterious but free unfolding of creation, however perplexing it may appear to us.

A God of Creation in Genesis

Biblical reflection on the creative action of God can be found in many traditions in the Hebrew and Christian Scriptures. This is not the place to rehearse them all. The best known of them, of course, are the passages found at the beginning of the Book of Genesis. These passages provide the narrative foundation for all subsequent biblical reflection upon creation and the *new* creation. Nowadays, interpreters of the Hebrew Bible are increasingly ignoring the apparently well-established and easily recognized "traditions" behind these early chapters. Not long ago the rhythmic telling of the seven days of creation belonged to one tradition (Gen 1:1—2:4a: the so-called Priestly tradition), and the more lively narrative of God's creation, including the vivid and fundamental stories that surround Adam and Eve and their offspring, belonged to another (2:4b—3:24: the so-called Yahwist tradition). There can be no denying that *both* the systematic telling of the days of creation (1:1—2:4a) and the vivid narratives of the chapters that follow (2:4b—3:24) wish to establish a truth fundamental to Jews and Christians: God is responsible for all creation, and anything he did was perfect. There is no place for chaos and disorder flowing directly from God's original creative activity. "In the beginning" there was the chaos of void (Gen 1:1–2), but then, "God said." God began to "say" things (1:3, 6, 9, 11, 14, 20, 24, 26, 29), and to create (1:3, 7, 9, 11, 15, 21, 24, 27). As creation unfolded, God "saw" that everything created was good (1:4, 12, 18, 21, 24, 31). However, as the original storytellers knew, and as all subsequent generations have come to accept on the basis of our experience of failure and suffering, disorder is now rampant, however "good" everything may have been at the beginning.

At this stage a closer look at the two accounts of creation in Genesis indicates that although these accounts reflect similarities, there

41

are important differences in approach to the goodness of God the creator and the role of human beings within that creation. In Gen 1:1—2:4a, God is always the main actor. God says, creates, sees, and approves. Man and woman are created only at the end of a long series of creative acts, on the sixth day (vv. 26–31). Made in the image of God, they are found at the apex of God's creative program, and all that has been created on the five previous days is given over to their care and use (vv. 28–30).

This first account of the creation reminds me of a Gothic cathedral. As you come through the main door, at the very front of the church, your eye is drawn up to vault after vault, each one a repetition of the same basic architectural features. But each one draws the eye further and further up the church, until it rests over the sanctuary. There the uplifting use of columns and ribbed walls and ceilings continues to draw the eye and the mind upward. In traditional European Gothic architecture, the final vault hovers over the high altar, often enshrining the tabernacle where, according to Catholic belief, the eucharistic presence of the risen Lord can be found. At each "vault" in the Genesis account, God sees that "it was good." But our translation of the Hebrew word *tôv* ("good") is too vague. The word carries the fuller meaning of "everything being the way it should be." God looks at the consequences of his creative word, and he sees that everything is the way he wants it to be! This expression is used five times. But on the sixth day, God creates man and woman and situates the results of each day in its correct relation with the whole of creation: he sees that it is *tôb meod* ("very good"; v. 31). The whole of creation, including each part's interlocking and mutually dependent relationships, is *exactly* the way God wants creation to be.

The creation poem tells of the culmination of God's creative intervention into what was only a formless mass (1:1–2). This beautiful text was no doubt written in a time of confusion and chaos, and the author wishes to proclaim that "in the beginning" things were not the way they are now. But—however chaotic the situation of the people for whom this poem was written—in this first account of the creation, there is no shadow of disaster, and no blame is imputed. Genesis 1:1—2:4a states a truth that must be kept alive in our discussions of natural disasters: God created all things, and he created them perfectly. No doubt the author of Genesis 1:1—2:4a lived in a world marked by sin and division, but he does not allow that experience to enter into his story of a perfect God creating a perfect universe.

Genesis 2:4b—3:24 tells a different tale. This vigorous narrative is an ongoing and sprawling saga of a relationship between God—who creates all things perfectly but wishes to establish a covenant of obedience—and the first of all men (*Adam*) and the first of all women (*Eve*). Adam and Eve disobey; they wish to make themselves "like God" (3:5, 22), and are thus punished (vv. 14–24). A mixture of many ancient narratives and more didactic traditions (especially genealogies) from Israel's past, Genesis 4–11 continues to focus upon human folly: Cain and Abel, the descendants of Adam, Noah and his sons, the tower of Babel. From the fall of Adam and Eve flows a stream of further blessings and subsequent failures until all human beings are scattered across the face of the earth, speaking different languages and thus unable to communicate with one another (Gen 11).

God enters this disastrous situation, created by human sinfulness, by calling Abraham, the father of Israel and of all the nations, in whom all nations will be blessed (12:1–3). That "calling" has led, through the biblical story, to Judaism's present way of life and its unquenchable hope. It led the Christian tradition into a belief that God's action in Abraham began a long history of salvation that was perfected in the obedience and the self-gift of Jesus of Nazareth (see Rom 4:1–25; Gal 3:1–20, 4:21—5:1; Heb 6:13—7:28). The major thrust of Genesis 2–3 is that God made all things exactly as they should be, including man and woman. But death and division had their origins in the disobedience and sinfulness of human beings, including the complex sexual tension between a woman and a man, now needing to cover themselves (3:21). The chaos and disaster, which the authors of Genesis 2–11 and all subsequent ages have experienced, are the result of human folly, disobedience, and sinfulness.

A necessary distinction between the questions raised by a religious person when faced by the devastations of natural disaster, and the more widespread presence of what has rightly been called "the sin of the world," can already be seen in the difference between these two creation accounts. Traditionally, Jews and Christians and Muslims, all of whom look back in different ways to these founding narratives, have explained the existence of evil in the world as the result of human sinfulness. God cannot and must not be blamed for *any* evil in the world, and that was why these narratives were written in the first place. The evil and chaos of the created world cannot be laid at God's door. Evil and its concomitant suffering have their origins and continue to spread like a disease because of the ever-increasing selfishness of human beings who still wish to "be like God" (3:5, 22).

Genesis's explanation of evil can be found only in chapters 3–11. There is no trace of it in Genesis 1:1—2:4a. It simply will not do to say that "somehow" human sinfulness is responsible for the apparent increase and immensity of natural disasters. So recourse to this traditional explanation of evil in the world is warranted. Powerful nations abuse the world's increasingly fragile ecological system for their own ends. But this line of argument should not be used to "explain away" the theological difficulties created by the biblical version of a perfect world created by a perfect God in Genesis 1:1—2:4a. The part of creation that we inhabit—the earth—seems to have a way of its own, and a will of its own, generating disasters that cannot be laid at the door of human evil. Many tragedies that take place in our small world *cannot be dismissed as the result of human sinfulness.* Nevertheless, a reading of Genesis as a whole can suggest that, while we must be aware that God's creation does not depend upon the human response, *set within the perfection and beauty of God's creation, human beings are free to accept or reject God, the creator.*

Creation in John and Paul

Interpreters of the Gospel of John have often seen the beginning of Jesus' story as driven by the theme of a "new creation." They come to this idea by adding up the number of days that pass in John 1:19–51, and arrive at a total of four days. Then they turn to John 2:1, and find that it begins with the words "On the third day there was a wedding in Cana in Galilee." Looking back to Genesis 1:1—2:4a, these interpreters suggest that the Gospel of John, like the Book of Genesis, also begins with seven days, and that both books open with "In the beginning." This proposal is attractive, but I do not find a lot of material in John 1:19—2:12 that deals with creation. It seems to deal more with the gradual self-revelation of Jesus to his disciples, leading to the promise of 1:51: "Very truly, I tell you, you will see heaven opened and the angels of God ascending and descending upon the Son of Man." The first moment of this "sight" is found in Jesus' manifestation of God's glory and the disciples' response to it in 2:11: "Jesus did this, the first of his signs, in Cana of Galilee, and revealed his glory; and his disciples believed in him." These first days of

Jesus' ministry may have more to do with *revelation* than with *creation*, and may be more closely associated with the days leading up to the gift of the Law to Moses on Sinai. This epoch-making moment in God's relationship with Israel also took place "on the third day" (see Exod 19:11, 15, 16), and the gift of the Law was regularly associated as a manifestation of "the glory of God" to Israel. In Exodus 19:16, the word for "thick clouds" in Hebrew (*ḳabôd*) also has the meaning of "glory," and is regularly interpreted that way in later Judaism.

Nevertheless John in 1:1–18, commonly known as the "Prologue" to the Gospel, makes an important contribution to developing Christian thinking about the role of the Word in creation. Although John never uses the expression *creation,* another way of presenting a *new creation* is found in his Gospel. In 1:3–4 a careful reader must face a punctuation question that influences one's interpretation. The manuscripts have no punctuation. We must provide it for our contemporary Greek texts and for our translations. In my understanding of this passage, we must read the original as follows: "All things came into being through him, and without him not one thing came into being" (v. 3). "What has come into being in him was life, and the life was the light of all people" (v. 3b, 4). The problematic punctuation causes difficulty, but problems for the interpreter are increased by John's threefold use of the same Greek verb *(ginomai)* in the two sentences. This verb is extremely versatile, and in John's first two uses of the verb it tells of the creative action of God that took place in the past: "in the beginning" (1:1). The verb is used in what is called the aorist tense, a verbal time that refers to events that have happened, once and for all, in the past. The whole of creation took place "through" the Word, and without the Word nothing came into being. Here the verb has the meaning of "to make, to bring into being."

The tense and the meaning change in verse 4! John uses the perfect tense, and the verb now ("come into being") has the meaning of "to happen, to take place." An event took place in the past, but that event has provided something that continues to affect us today. That is the way the Greeks used the perfect tense. If I were writing Greek to tell of a home I built for my family thirty years ago that still stood as the center of all that we were and did together, I would have to use the perfect tense. In my opinion, verse 4 is not about God's first creative act, but about what Paul calls the "new creation": the saving presence of the Word among us, although John's understanding of this creative act is more closely associated with the revelation of love than with Jesus' obedience. Of course, the two are not far apart. Everything that happened in and through the salvific presence of the Word among us was life, and the life was the light of humankind. What took place in the incarnation (v. 14) remains among us as life and light.

For the moment, let us focus our attention on John's affirmation: "All things came into being through him (Greek: *di'autou*), and without him not one thing came into being" (v. 3ab). Looking back to a tradition already well established within the Wisdom traditions of Jewish thought (especially Wisdom and Proverbs), John regards the Word of God that in loving union has been turned toward God from before all time (1:1–2) as both the *reason for* and the *model of* all creation (vv. 3–4a). There is a union between God and the Word so intimate that what God is, the Word also is (see v. 1c). This means that the creation of the world is both directed by a divine model, the Word, and aimed at receiving the divine, the Word. Later in the Prologue, we will learn that this Word has entered the human story, and his name is Jesus Christ (1:14, 16–17). The perfection, the beauty, indeed the divine nature of creation spelled out by these terse words in the Johannine Prologue recall the teaching of Genesis 1:1—2:4a. There can be no doubt about the intimate involvement of God, and the presence of the divine, within the created world. For Genesis, this was indicated by God's decision to make the creation of man and woman in the image of God (Gen 1:26–27) the culminating element in the systematic transformation of chaos into all that was "good." Although not close to the intentions of the Johannine author, there is a certain sense in which the final establishment of God's created order in the human couple of woman and man, made in the image of God, "divinized" the human. Through John's use of the Wisdom traditions, and his passionate belief in the presence of the divine in Jesus Christ, he has developed this image into a startling claim: God has charged the whole universe with a divinity that reflects through whom and for whom it came into being— the Word (1:3ab). The Word became flesh and took up a dwelling among us, and that person was named Jesus Christ (1:14, 17).

We saw in our reading of Genesis 1–3 (and indeed, Gen 1–11) that the majestic description of the perfect creation generated by the word of God runs into a more dramatic encounter between God and human beings, whom God creates with a freedom to accept or refuse his word. In the case of Adam and Eve, it was a word that prohibited their eating the fruit of the tree of good and evil (Gen 2:15–17). In their

God-given freedom, they rejected God's word and suffered the consequences. A parallel message is found later in the Johannine Prologue.
John returns to the theme of creation in verse 10: "He was in the world,
and the world came into being *through him*" (Greek: *di'autou*, recalling
exactly the same expression used of God's creation through the Word
in v. 3ab). But the rest of the passage establishes that "the world" is free
to choose. It can reject or accept what God has done in and through his
creation: "...the world did not know him. He came to what was his
own, and his own people did not accept him. But to all who received
him, who believed in his name, he gave power to become children of
God" (vv. 10c–12).

Already in his Prologue, the author of the Fourth Gospel states
one of the fundamental themes of his Gospel: a God who created and
loved the world has made himself known in and through Jesus, but that
invitation can be accepted or rejected. Acceptance leads to life, and rejection leads to death (see especially 3:16–21, but the theme can be found
throughout the Gospel and the Johannine Epistles). At the end of Jesus'
public ministry, the author comments on why "the Jews" did not accept
Jesus. Playing upon the double meaning of the Greek word *doxa*, which
can mean human success and privilege, or the revelation of God (see 2:11),
the author states: "For they loved human glory (*doxa*) more than the glory
(*doxa*) that comes from God" (12:43). As with Genesis, and the biblical
story that builds upon it, human beings are free to reject God, and chaos
and suffering flow from that rejection. But again I must insist—*this is not
the case with natural disasters.* Our analysis of the Johannine teaching on
creation, however, leaves us with a conclusion that parallels one of the
results of our earlier reading of Genesis: *set within the perfection and beauty
of God's creation, human beings are free to accept or reject God, the creator.*

The teaching of the apostle Paul is dominated by the cross and
resurrection of Jesus. He does not tell the story of Jesus' death and resurrection (but see 1 Cor 11:23–25 and 15:1–8 for references to it). He sets the
drama of what God has done for humankind in and through Jesus within
the broader canvas of a traditional Jewish view of history. For Jewish
thought at the time of Paul, the human story began with a brief era of
glory, but fell into chaos as a result of the radical disobedience generated
by Adam's sin (see Rom 5:12). For Paul, this chaos was not resolved by the
gift of the Law. The Law made it possible to know sin, and to strain to
avoid sin, but the Law could not save from the pains and anguish of the

disobedience to God that which entered the human story through Adam (see Rom 7:1–25). The original glory, for Jewish thought, would return only at the end of all time. At the *end of all history*, when God would return to restore the whole of his original creation in its beauty, and to destroy all evil, the situation that marked *the beginning of all history* would return. The end of all time would be the same as the beginning of all time. As the Germans say in a synthetic fashion that is uniquely part of the German mindset, *Endzeit=Urzeit* ("end time=original time"). In this scheme we find a notion unique to the Jewish and biblical tradition: the creation itself is of God, marked by the harmony and peace that reflect God's perfection. Such glory was present at the beginning, and it will return at the end.

But for Paul, the death and resurrection of Jesus interrupted this scheme by anticipating the possibility of glory. In Jesus' unconditional *obedience* to God, the situation of Adam's *disobedience* was reversed. Not even Jesus' being God's Son could prevent his obedient acceptance of the cross. This obedience led to the resurrection, Jesus' exaltation and his establishment as Lord in the presence of God (see Phil 2:6–11). This action *took place in human history*. One of us, the man Jesus Christ, *reversed* Adam's situation, and made it possible, *already within human history*, to be filled with the Spirit and to cry out to God as Father and Lord (see Gal 4:4–7). For Paul, the believer must "put on Christ" (see Gal 3:27). We no longer live ourselves, but Christ lives in us. The life we now live in the flesh we live by faith in the Son of God, who loved us and gave himself for us (see Gal 2:20). This means that the believer accepts the grace God freely offers, to live and die as Jesus did in radical obedience to God, and in this way belongs to a "new creation" (Gal 6:15; 2 Cor 5:17). Paul adheres to the Jewish tradition that God created all things perfectly, and that this perfection—however it may now appear to be under the sway of sin—will return at the end of time. However, in the meantime, a "new creation" is available, drawing the promise of the final glory into human history. For that reason Christian believers can be called an "eschatological people." While living in this world, they are already partially enjoying some of the fruits of the end-time; they live the "in between" time, between the glory of their lives in Christ *now*, and the final establishment of God's glory at the end of all time.

What I have sketched in the previous paragraph can be found behind every page of the Pauline Epistles. Again, however, a theme common to both Genesis and the Gospel of John emerges. God is the creator, and his creation is perfect. For Paul and John, the only way to restore the promises of the original creative act of God is through belief and acceptance of Jesus. Paul and John say it in their own way, and the nuances are important. For Paul, however, as for John, *human beings are free.* Jesus' life, death, and resurrection have rewritten human history: the story of Adam's disobedience, forever plunging humankind into chaos and sin, has been overcome by the story of Jesus' obedience to the Father. *Both stories—that of Adam and that of Christ—are present in the world.* Human beings must make a choice. To which story do they wish to adhere? For the reader of this essay, Paul's understanding of human history is probably most conveniently summed up in Romans 5:12–21, in which he sets out the two choices, convinced that only by inserting ourselves into the story of Jesus can we become part of the "new creation," members of God's eschatological people.

This passage in Roman's should be read in its entirety, but Paul's convictions are clear: "For if the many died through the one man's trespass, much more surely have the grace of God and the free gift in the grace of the one man, Jesus Christ, abounded for the many.... If, because of the one man's trespass, death exercised dominion through that one, much more surely will those who receive the abundance of grace and the free gift of righteousness exercise dominion in life through the one man, Jesus Christ.... For just as by the one man's disobedience the many were made sinners, so by the one man's obedience the many will be made righteous" (5:15, 17, 19). Paul has generated this remarkable rhetoric to sway his readers. He starts with the conviction that they are free to accept or reject the gift of God that is made available through Jesus Christ. As with Genesis and the Gospel of John, so also with Paul: *set within the perfection and beauty of God's creation, and the possibility of a "new creation," human beings are free to accept or reject God the creator and the saving obedience of his Son, Jesus Christ.* For Paul, as with John, God's saving creative act does not take place *only* at the end of time. It takes place in and through all time through the person of Jesus.

A Cosmic Freedom?

Our selected biblical reflection to this point has described the already well known: God created a perfect world, marked by harmony, peace, love, and right order. God also created men and women who are free to accept or reject what God has offered in his original creation and, for Christian authors, in the new creation that takes place in and through Jesus Christ. At this point in the reflection, some speculation based upon the biblical data may take us further and lead to a conclusion on the presence or absence of God in natural disasters. It has rightly been said that human beings are the greatest of God's creatures because they have been gifted with *unconditioned freedom.* We are summoned by God, in many and varied ways, to live our freedom in accord with God's design, set out for us in his original creation, and—for Christians—carried deeper into the mystery of human experience in and through Jesus Christ. *But we do not have to accept that summons.* This much is amply exemplified for us in the biblical material we have considered above. We are not marionettes, little wooden dolls that respond to God's string-pulling from outside the stage of human history. Nowhere in the biblical traditions, either Hebrew or Christian, does the image appear of a God who directs human lives by "pulling strings." God may often get the blame for human tragedy, but the Bible makes it clear that such chaos is generated by human freedom.

It is almost a platitude that the hallmark of the human condition is freedom. Men and women are made that way, and they suffer intensely in those situations in which they are deprived of freedom. But what can one say of the rest of the created world? A very brief passage in Genesis 3 suggests that, despite Genesis 1:28–30 in which creation is given into the hands of women and men, the animate and inanimate worlds are neither subjected to the will and purpose of humankind, nor directed by the extraterrestrial "strings of God." Spelling out the consequences of sin, God tells the man and the woman that the original perfect union between humankind, the animals, and the inanimate world has been broken. From this point on, humankind will find that the animal world will turn against its former master, a woman must bear children in pain, and the earth will resist being "used" by human beings, who must now work against its rebellion by the sweat of their brows (Gen 3:14–19). It appears that *the whole of creation has a will of its own*, no longer subjected to God's original design, where everything was marked by harmony.

Another consideration, which I can only raise here in passing, is the immensity of God's creation. I have neither the skills nor the space to develop this thought, but it must not be left unstated. There is an arrogance about the human being, the intelligent inhabitants and lords of the planet called Earth, who tends to regard God as only concerned with *this* planet and the events that happen here. Earth, its inhabitants, and the interrelationship between the human, the animal, and the inanimate world—all of it is only a microcosm of God's larger creation. The whole universe, much of which still lies outside the reach of the human mind and its technology, continues to spin through time and space, *following its own laws.* As God created the tiny creature called the human being and gave it *freedom*, is it not true that God also created the entire universe and set it *free* to pursue its own order, its own history, and to work out the complex interrelationships that exist across that universe?

Natural disasters are called "disasters" because of what they do to upset the right order of the human condition, as we understand it and as we have constructed it. Cities are destroyed, thousands are injured or die, economies are left in tatters, all because creation seems to have a will of its own. What appeared to be ordered—just the perfect place for an idyllic holiday on a tropical beach—becomes a killer. The creation does not behave as we expect it to behave.

We accept that the *gift of freedom* marked God's creation of the human being. Should we not also accept that the *gift of freedom* also marked God's creation of the universe? Limited as we are in what we know of the universe as a whole, we can still suggest that the human being who lives on earth is specially privileged. From the start, man and woman are given *intellectual freedom*, and it is within the human story that God has loved us so much that he gave us his only Son (see John 3:16). When I write of *the freedom* of the rest of creation, I do not wish to draw any sort of parallel between human freedom and the freedom of the rest of creation. On the basis of the biblical record, that would be an outlandish claim.

What I wish to claim, on the basis of the biblical record, is that the whole universe has God at its beginnings. When, how, and what that means is open to every kind of scientific investigation and theory. Never did the poets and theologians that produced the creation narratives in the Book of Genesis wish to suggest they had an answer to the many scientific and theological issues that still rage over this issue, from big bang theory to intelligent design. There must be no straitjacketing of creation into something *we can explain*, theologically or scientifically. That is another act of human arrogance, as it attempts to explain away the mystery of God and God's impenetrable action. But the created world runs according to *its agenda.* If we can rightly claim that God does not intervene in human history by means of a controlling hand, but allows human history to run its own course as we exercise our freedom, can we not claim that something parallel takes place with the rest of creation?

Conclusion

The world as we know it certainly follows its own "rules." It would be impossible to live in this world if that were not the case. In human society we attempt to establish authorities to see that rules are followed, and to control and even punish those who will not live according to them. But God—present at the beginning of creation, throughout the history of creation, the goal toward which creation moves—does not intervene. He is watching us, with great care and attention, but from a distance. Similarly, the rest of the created world follows its own "rules," and scientists of many disciplines are still struggling to determine what those rules are. Only *after* the tsunami were we educated to the not-unexpected effects of shifts in the earth's fragile crust deep in the sea that naturally produce massive and destructive waves. What happened was perfectly explainable, and even to be expected. But when faced with natural disaster, we have no tribunal to which we can call the perpetrator of the devastating events. This frustrates human beings, who long to be able to locate blame, and in this frustration, "the God question" emerges. Whom else can we blame?

As God does not intervene to direct human history, nor does God intervene to direct the vicissitudes of the rest of creation as it works out its own history, following its own rules. Frustrated by our inability to call nature to task, however, and to completely dominate it by our wills and our agendas, when nature unexpectedly asserts itself, *we blame God.* We know that natural disasters can and will happen, as nature responds to its own "rules," but we live as if we did not know. The lack of preparation for the arrival of Hurricane Katrina, and the negligence of the poor during and after that tragedy, is eloquent proof that such is the case.

To ask why God lets this happen and what sort of God lies behind such destruction and suffering is to ask the wrong questions. As God made us free, God also made the created universe free. We are made to follow our own histories and to follow our own "rules" until we all finally rest in God. There are times when human history and the history of the rest of creation intersect violently, but such events are the result of God's greatest gift to the whole of creation: *freedom*, a freedom enjoyed by both human beings and the rest of the universe, however differently these freedoms work themselves out.

We do not believe in a God who manipulates creation. Our biblical faith insists that God is intimately involved in the created world, and that traces of the divine can be found there. We further believe in a God who so loved the world that he gave us his only son (John 3:16), so that we may love one another as he has loved us (13:34–35; 15:12, 17). We are not *forced* into such acts of love, but we are summoned by the Word of God, especially as it has been lived, taught, and manifested in the death and resurrection of Jesus, to give ourselves *freely* over to such loving. As God watches and cares for us, we sometimes respond to *God's design* rather than our own, when nature expresses its violent potential, and tragedy strikes the human village. As God watches—it is in those moments that we often find harmony, the voice of hope and the voice of peace, the voice of every human being…so patently absent in our otherwise publicly corrupt and war-ravaged first decade of the third millennium.

Questions for Reflection

1. Why is it that the "God question" emerges from natural disasters and subsequent evil, while it seldom emerges from the evil that flows from human sin?
2. Is the presence of the divine in the world clouded by natural disasters? Why?
3. Does faith in God's final restoration of the beauty of all that was made help in a Christian understanding of natural disasters?
4. Can you accept that creation must follow "its own rules"?

5

Why Have You Abandoned Us?
Liturgy in Time of Natural Disaster
Richard E. McCarron

To seek God in time of natural disaster summons for me the anguished cry of the psalmist that we hear during Holy Week and that is put on the lips of the dying Jesus on the cross in the Gospels of Mark and Matthew: "My God, my God, why have you forsaken me? Why are you so far from helping me, from the words of my groaning?" (Ps 22:1). This visceral and honest reaction then launches a plea to God—a lament—that allows protest, memory, and hope to intersect. Liturgy in time of disaster can help the community make that same plea, unite that plea with the Church's memory and hope in the Paschal Mystery of Christ, and then move forward beyond that plea to remember the Body of Christ: to bind the wounds of injury and grief, to gather the scattered, and to hold the dead in communion.

The reflections that follow are grounded in two convictions that must remain presuppositions for what I am going to share. The first conviction is that the ways in which the Church prays, believes, and lives are mutually connected, though how we work that out in any given moment remains under negotiation. The second conviction is that our liturgical worship is a privileged moment in which scripture, theology, pastoral care, and ethics are integrated. Again, what gets integrated and how well it is integrated also remain an ongoing challenge.

So because of this interplay of prayer, belief, and life, liturgy may well be the primary event in which a community in time of disaster grapples with its identity in Christ, its belief, and its commitment to others. This exploration will first consider what has been and is in the Church's official liturgical repertoire for a time of natural disaster and what that says about who God is for us. Then, I turn to alternatives to that repertoire, with particular attention to the role of lament. After presenting some basic principles for liturgy in time of natural disaster, I offer an outline for a liturgy that may spark the imagination of local churches faced with the difficult task of preparing worship in the wake of ravages of earth, sea, and sky.

Catholic Liturgical Repertoire, Past and Present

It should come as no surprise that our forebears also sought God, in local and more-or-less organized ways, in times of natural disaster. The history of liturgy helps us to appreciate some of those strategies that are at least "on the books" today. A quick glance at how the Church has organized liturgical response to disaster shows two particular forms that were initiated locally and then became part of the official Roman Missal in due course and with new inflection: litanies in procession and the celebration of Masses for various needs.

The first liturgical response, litanies in procession, has two sources. The first, from the local Church of Rome in the late fourth century, came to be known as the "greater litanies" and was the Church's adaptation of the Roman custom of imploring the god of mildew to protect the fields of grain from blight. Celebrated on April 25 (later to be designated the feast of St. Mark), the greater litanies were suppressed with the calendar reform of Vatican II.

The second source, from fifth-century Gaul (present-day France), was known as the "lesser litanies" or rogations, and emerged in response to a series of natural disasters. (Rogation comes from the Latin verb *rogare*, "to ask for"; many people will remember the pre–Vatican II "Rogation Days.") The people fasted and then processed with the singing of litanies to ward off impending or future danger, and later also to recall deliverance from some particular harm. For example, the procession to avert a storm came to consist of singing the litany of the saints in procession (with a special invocation recited twice: "From lightning and storm, deliver us, Lord") followed by the Lord's Prayer, Psalm 147:12–20 ("Praise the Lord, O Jerusalem!"), verses and responses, and a series of Collects, concluded by a sprinkling with holy water (*Rituale Romanum*, title 9).

The *Commentary on the General Norms for the Liturgical Year and Calendar* (1975) notes that Rogation Days are to be retained, explaining that their observance is most appropriately determined by the conference of bishops of the region (2.VII.46). The norms envision not only the immediate need, but a memorial of times of distress as well. However, the current Missal does not provide a specific order for them, and examples of them as memorials are relatively few. Rogations have generally not been retrieved or adapted to contemporary situations. The practice of litanies in procession calls attention to the ritual elements of place and movement, responsive forms, the role of psalms, and an accent on intercession. Traditionally the Penitential Psalms (6, 32, 38, 51, 102, 130, and 143) and the litany of the saints came to form an important repertoire for expressing not only sorrow but also lament and intercession in time of need or anguish.

The second liturgical response to natural disasters is the practice of votive Masses. The proliferation of texts for Masses for particular needs, especially through the Middle Ages, reveals a number of Collects for the natural disasters that befell our forebears—drought, flood, or the plague, for example. The current Roman Missal continues to offer prayers for certain natural disasters—famine, earthquake, drought, storms, and so on.

There is a particular theology at work in these prayers that is worth some reflection. They invoke God as almighty, eternal, and omnipotent, the one whom all the elements obey. God is also invoked as involved in the well-being of creation, acting with mercy and providing protection. The relationship of human creatures to their Creator is typical of the way that the classical Roman liturgy prayed: we human beings entreat and supplicate with humility, sometimes with penitence. As petitioners we ask God to be present to us. Yet because of God's power, might, and mercy, we are confident to come before God in our time of need. At times the prayers reflect a deeply biblical sentiment, like that of Psalm 147:

> [God] sends out his command to the earth;
>> his word runs swiftly.
> He gives snow like wool;
>> he scatters frost like ashes.
> He hurls down hail like crumbs—
>> who can stand before his cold?

He sends out his word, and melts them;
he makes his wind blow, and the waters flow.
(Ps 147:15–18)

Many of the prayers offer rationale for why we should be spared menace and danger: that we may serve God anew with praise and rejoicing. We ask God that we may be relieved and restored so that we can be ever more devoted in service of God. The prayer for the time of earthquake shows these movements:

God,
who established the earth on its firm foundation,
spare the fearful and heed the petitioner
that, the danger of an earthquake having thoroughly
    been removed,
we may feel your mercy unceasingly
and, safe by your protection,
we may serve you rejoicing.

Missale Romanum

However, the people's actual experience in a time of disaster puts some questions to the theology of these prayers. The prayers contain no protesting, no wondering why we are afflicted, no questioning if God is present in the time of need. In the prayers of the Missal, the petitions are less for immediate needs than for more generalized spiritual ends. The Collects are also primarily concerned with current situations, and there are no texts for the commemoration of a disaster.

There is further concern. For some in the midst of recovery from disaster, the celebration of Mass with its chants of Alleluia and Holy, holy might well be premature, from a psychological perspective. Liturgists and pastoral theologians have made use of the late Elisabeth Kübler-Ross's stages of dying to point also to the stages of *dealing* with death and tragedy. Celebration of the Eucharist ("thanksgiving") might also be more appropriate *after* some time has passed and the stage of acceptance reached. This may be necessitated locally in the face of devastation, but it may also be that we historically have tended to move to thanksgiving too quickly and have not allowed adequate time for the expression of anger, exasperation, grief, mourning, and lament.

My God! My God?

Perhaps, then, liturgy needs to be open to seeking God in new ways in the time of natural disaster. Through the passing of time, what can be named as "emergent" ritual in times of disaster has sounded a critique of the official liturgical texts and rites. Something more is needed. The events and experiences of people continue to call for an evaluation of the liturgical orders. The whole spectrum of human emotions will be at play: For some, relief and rejoicing that they have survived without bump or bruise, their belongings and place they call home intact. For others, physical pain and emotional anguish in the face of injury and loss. For still others, numbing grief and disconsolate tears mourning their beloved who have been killed. Throughout these currents may flow anger, disbelief, and despair as well as courage, hope, and fortitude.

In response to the experience of natural disaster and an authentic way of responding to God in such times, new patterns of worship will need to emerge. The celebration of votive Masses has its place, and penitential processions like rogations have a purpose, but they bear the marks of the theology of a particular period and of the liturgical expression that served at that time. However, they do not exhaust how Catholic Christians today can, through liturgy, look for God and respond to God in time of natural disaster. Christian liturgy must always be timely. There is no single universal response to some generic natural disaster; rather, we need a plurality of ways of dealing with very particular experiences of events unique to a local church. We do well to pay attention to emerging rituals and examples of liturgical improvisation at the same time as we need to retrieve lament.

Emerging Rituals

Before a community might even come together for official worship after a natural disaster, liturgy is already taking place—the liturgy of the world and of the people's own rites. It is important to keep in mind that these spontaneous rites intersect before, during, and after any official response of the Church. There is the relief effort both of the local community and of those who have traveled great lengths to help, whether out of a sense of duty or of compassion for the victims and survivors. There is the burial of the dead, the urgency for which and the sheer numbers involved may not allow for official funeral rites. There are the prayers and memorials both inside and outside the church—if a building is left.

People today, specifically in a U.S. context, draw from the multiple sources of their social, cultural, and religious identity in a time of crisis. They engage in a creative blending of available elements to fashion a rite to respond to this new situation. These elements are borrowed from family, from local communities, from cultural heritage, from Catholic experience, and from wider U.S. society. These often exist side by side with their involvement in official Church liturgy. One can go to church to light a candle, then head to Ground Zero to place another candle or a picture, a saying, or a bouquet of flowers after walking in a procession. In the United States, the now-obligatory memorial service will cut and paste ritual elements and words from various traditions, together with secular pomp and entertainment-industry ceremony. Years after the media frenzy in the actual time of natural disaster come the local memorial events, where the naming of those who have perished is the root ritual action. Even many more years away is the memorial or monument or museum that will be built—whether by the small town or the country where the event has happened.

There has emerged a new repertoire of ritual elements that are fast becoming part of the strategies of worship in time of disaster, as fluid as they must be. These include lighting candles, placing pictures and other material reminders, reading poetry, giving testimony, wearing a ribbon or flower or specially made button, performing local music, even marking the resumption of normal routine with ritual attention. While there is a certain futility in trying to make these spontaneous popular expressions into an official event, if the popular does not inform the official it will be hollow. These liturgies may be celebrated only once, but their celebration will leave a lasting imprint in the memory of the community. It will be recalled and evoked both in day-to-day narrative and at formal events.

The history of liturgy demonstrates that at times the people kept authentic memorial of the Christ's Paschal Mystery, not through participation in Mass or the Liturgy of the Hours, but through their own rites and prayers. This issue is balance. With time, many of these popular rites have informed the official liturgy of the Church, which became ever more enriched through them. The celebration of the Liturgy of the

Hours (the office of readings or evening prayer) or Liturgy of the Word, being more flexible than the Order of Mass, might provide a frame into which the popular elements can be grafted. But by definition, *popular* does not mean "what most folk like to do"; it means those rituals that remain out of the control of official specialists, perhaps for good reason. We need both—official and popular. We need to explore our own capacity for creativity in rituals.

Lament

If there is another capacity that needs to be stretched, it is the recovery of the practice of lament—not only in terms of psalmody in a given order of worship, but more so as a way to order worship itself. There is still deep need for Christians to learn what it means "when to worship is to lament," in the words of theologian David Power.

Historically, the Roman Liturgy seems to have little in terms of lament in prayer genres and poetry other than the use of individual and communal lament psalms or of readings from the Book of Lamentations in Holy Week. Mostly, however, the practice of lament survived on the margins of liturgy, not in the center. Lament came to reside in the realm of popular religiosity, specifically manifesting itself during Holy Week, when the faithful would enact the lament and grief of the Sorrowful Mother, and at death, like the Celtic tradition of keening, as well as other cultures' practice of mourning and lamenting the dead. In the Byzantine tradition, lament features in the funeral liturgy, for example, in the haunting hymns of St. John Damascene, and also in the liturgies celebrated during Holy Week, especially Great (Good) Friday evening.

While lament psalms continue to be used, it is unlikely that most folks in the pew today are aware of the movements of lament, especially because of their infrequent exposure to praying entire psalms. Old Testament scholar Walter Brueggemann has perhaps been the most recognizable and eloquent voice for retrieving the vital practice of lament based on the genre of the psalms. Brueggemann names the "costly loss of lament" in the Church—a community diminished in its covenant partnership with God. Lament enables a community to protest and question God's involvement, invoke God's salvific intervention, redress relationships, and keep the question of justice alive. Only out of lament can authentic thanksgiving and praise emerge, argues Brueggemann.

While there are, of course, many nuances and particularities among the psalms of lament or complaint, both communal and individual, Old Testament scholar Claus Westermann's pattern, or movement, for lament in the psalms remains helpful for our purposes here:

1. Address to God (with introductory petition)
2. Complaint or lament
3. Confession of trust
4. Petition for help
5. Words of assurance
6. Vow of praise

What Brueggemann and others argue is that Westermann's pattern is not just a particular way of arranging a song, but rather a strategic way of engaging God in human emotion and covenant relationship. As many others have suggested, this pattern can serve as a shape for worship to help people understand the deep dynamics of lament. A liturgy whose order follows the movements of lament can help shape people to learn this practice so that they might come to embody these movements whenever tragedy strikes. Unlike the Roman Collect prayer-form, or the order of the Liturgy of the Word, this pattern allows space for the community to protest, to complain, and to register its plea before God—even to question where God is in the midst of mud and muck. The confession of trust takes the form of narrative remembrance of how God has acted in steadfast love in mercy, as well as how the people may have strayed. Or it can take the form of the people's fidelity and a protest that *God* seems to have strayed, even though God promised to be steadfast mercy and compassion.

This narrative memorial summons God back to the center of our time and our space where God seems to be absent. The petition for help is not left echoing across a scorched field or a torn landscape, but is met with the words of assurance—the hope with which Christians should grieve, as St. Paul exhorted. Only then, against this setting of protest, petition, and assurance, does the vow of praise or thanksgiving emerge. It may or may not be immediate; it may take some people some time—but only out of lament is true praise sung. And like any vow taken, it involves the whole self and a promise of bodily action as well as mental assent. This genre of liturgical lament holds the possibility of transforming people in situations of chaos and loss because of its honesty to human emotion and the depth of covenant relationship with God on which it is grounded.

Shaping a Liturgical Response: Some Principles

Any liturgical response must be local. There will be a need for provisions for liturgy in the face of natural disaster, whether it is forecasted, like a hurricane, or imminent, like the steady burn of wildfires borne by capricious winds. Liturgy will be needed in the aftermath of the event, including the days and weeks of recovery. Spontaneous tributes and memorial services for the dead will also be offered. For those assemblies of Christians removed geographically from the event, there will be need for liturgy in solidarity with those afflicted. And in due course, liturgy will be needed to mark the memorial of the event and those who died.

Those who have the awesome and perhaps overwhelming responsibility to prepare any one of these liturgies should take into consideration some principles to ground their work or to help in evaluating resources available to them. The speed of the Internet can make posting suggested liturgies very convenient, but the need for careful theological and liturgical consideration of these resources is perhaps even more acute when dealing with disaster. The following seven points are intended to help guide that reflection. These principles are primarily oriented to local liturgies in the aftermath of a natural disaster, liturgies in solidarity in a time of disaster, and memorial events. They apply both to the liturgical order as well as to the preaching that might take place.

Preparing for a multiplicity of people's responses

Certain liturgies try to corral all the participants into a single narrative, a single expression of emotion, or a single image of God. Such a liturgy risks being irrelevant, or worse, coercive. Be especially aware that there will be a multiplicity of responses to the event and that the person who wants to sing alleluia to God might be next to the person who wants to curse God. The liturgical assembly should embrace both and needs both to speak authentically. Start with the people and not with preconceived notions of what is "supposed be happening." This requires a listening ear and an open heart to what is going on in the local community. It requires a range of ritual elements—silence, words, gestures, music, and other symbols—that reflect the range of human emotion and faith response.

Naming God and grace

Perhaps nowhere is the interplay of praying and believing more acutely at work than in the face of natural disaster, illness, and death. More acutely, these may be times when one's faith in God and one's understanding of who God is can be utterly shattered. This is a vulnerable time. We have to be honest that for us as ministers and for all who gather, there is a theology at work. In times of crisis, we must be humble enough to question its adequacy and willing to engage in other ways of thinking and talking about God. Simply put, a liturgy will look very different if we put the blame at God's feet or our feet or FEMA's feet. A liturgy will sound very different if we are more schooled in thanksgiving than in the ache of lament. A liturgy will resonate in very different ways if we have hope in God or if we are so stung by the event that we have given up on God. Liturgy is theology and ecclesiology in action; it can be more or less adequate for the community gathered, but it is never neutral.

Claiming, disclaiming, or reclaiming symbols

Liturgy makes use of natural symbols as its primary way to touch the human heart and imagination. Liturgical theologians speak of liturgy as being parabolic—that is, it takes the daily, ordinary things of life and turns them around in the name of Christ and the power of the Spirit to point to something radically new: immersion in water is rebirth, fire is Christ our Light, bread is the Body of Christ, night and day are the participation in a daily dying and rising in Christ, wind is the breath of the Spirit of Creation. But in time of natural disaster—water and air in a flood or hurricane, fire and earth in time of earthquake or wildfire, ash in a volcano blast, bread and wine in time of famine—these symbols of life-giving power are trumped, overturned, and perhaps even forever broken. Yet new symbols can emerge from the experience of survival in the face of destruction: the splinters of the town meeting hall, a ring or locket found in the mud, a façade that survived unscathed, the charred but still recognizable teddy bear. And the spontaneous memorials might offer even more: lamps, candles, flowers, scribbled notes, pictures. Liturgy in time of disaster must be unusually sensitive to the complex symbolic field. And it must take risks. Drawing on French Jesuit Joseph Gelineau, American liturgical scholar Janet Walton says that we need to be able to throw symbols to people. Some may catch them and hold them tight. Others might drop them looking for something else that actually touches their heart. Still others might throw them out in disgust or even back at us in a fit of rage.

Does the liturgy need to make use of water to name it again as a source of rebirth and forgiveness and renewal? Does it need stones and an empty cup to lament the lack of food? Does it need ash and dust and dirt to be rejected rather than blessed? Does it need to offer fire to be both kindled and extinguished while calling on the name of God? Does it need to let people touch the surviving beam of the town hall after a tornado and to breathe on it, whether in hope in a steadfast God or in defiance of the Spirit of Creation?

Note that in all of these cases people are engaged with symbols, not words. The process of claiming, disclaiming, and reclaiming symbols means relinquishing our preoccupation with words and more words to explain and comment at every turn in a liturgy. Let the symbols speak instead, and to do so, silence is needed.

Balancing order and spontaneity

Because many ministers are so used to liturgies that are clearly ordered and allow little if any room for people to say or do anything that has not been scripted, the very idea of spontaneity is unwelcome to them. However, in times of disaster, there needs to be a balance of order and spontaneity in both large and small group settings. In many cultures, spontaneity is expected. In times of disaster, it seems to me to be demanded cross-culturally. In shock, grief, and anxiety there should be ample time for both silence and testimony. The order of the prayer should offer room to interact with any symbols as the participants are moved to assume different postures—sitting, standing, kneeling, prostrating. The space created for worship should be experienced as a place of safety, respect, and retreat.

A time of natural disaster summons up deep feelings of vulnerability, fragility, and uncertainty. The liturgy should allow for the raw feelings to be expressed; it should also offer comfort and assurance in a way that takes the raw feelings seriously and doesn't erase them with quick happy faces. Christian comfort and assurance are rooted in the Paschal Mystery of Christ, not in contemporary America's culture—its "sunshine and happy days" myth of health and wealth. We should also recall the wail heard in the city of Ramah, "lamentation and bitter weeping [because] Rachel is weeping for her children; she refuses to be comforted for her children, because they are no more" (Jer 31:15).

Leaning into lament

This proposition will take many out of their comfort zones, as well it should. We are very comfortable with giving God all the praise, but we are not as well rehearsed in the practice of lament. Lament enables us to look death and destruction in the face, not to turn away. It enables us to engage the awful ache rather than ignore it. Our personal struggle is brought to bear on communal memory, and the communal memory and hope permeate our individual lament. As the psalms of lament show, and as St. Paul exhorted, we do not grieve like those without hope. Lament is rooted in the covenant relationship and sustained by hope and trust in God, even in the experience of abandonment. The cry of Jesus on the cross from Psalm 22 gives us a model of protest and his story the consolation of hope: he broke the chains of death, smashed the doors of hell, and rose again: death has no more power over us. This does not mean that we do not grieve, for we indeed feel the sting of death. But we do not grieve like those who have no hope. Notice that lament is not just about *naming* grief, pain, and loss, but about taking them head on and *struggling* with them in light of God's promise. Lament's language is more poetry than prose. It touches our hearts and minds with its poignancy and beauty. The poetry of lament is more apt than prose to express grief, pain, and loss. Helping us to resist explaining them away, lament holds them open for us to contemplate their complexity and depth.

In leaning into lament, we might also recognize that just as it is a process that unfolds, so too our liturgies might be a process. Rather than just one isolated event, our liturgical observance might be spread out over a day or a week and may perhaps give rise to regular gatherings in remembrance. This might be the best way to incorporate the celebration of the Eucharist. Perhaps the leaders might envision, for the morning, a gathering for procession that leads to a liturgy of testimony, lament, and petition. Then, later that day, there is an evening prayer to remember the dead and seek assurance. The following morning the celebration of Eucharist can constitute our vow of praise.

Letting the liturgy be liturgy

Liturgy, in its most tangible, is the embodied, corporate, ritual prayer of the Church locally gathered. These celebrations manifest, theologically speaking, at a fundamental dimension, humankind's participation in the eternal liturgy of life of the Trinity: the rhythmic dance of love of the Holy Three in One. In turn our celebrations here and now, which share in the eternal liturgy, flow from and lead to the "liturgy of the world," that potential experience each day of encounter with God in love and our self-offering to God and neighbor. As Vatican II's *Constitution on the Sacred Liturgy* emphasizes, there is a threefold purpose to celebration: the sanctification of humankind, the building up of the Body of Christ, and the worship of God (no. 59). At liturgy's center is the celebration of the Paschal Mystery of Christ (no. 5).

There is a great temptation these days to overlay liturgy with multiple agendas and themes. Often this comes from a desire to reach people while you have them, but it almost always distorts common worship. Neither in the midst of disaster recovery nor in solidarity with those who suffer should liturgy become a "teachable moment." Certainly liturgy has a power to form people, but it does so in complex ways through bodily gestures and postures, through poetic word, through central symbols, and through music and environment. This is not the time for catechetical explanations, didactic exhortations, or sermons on theodicy. Likewise, liturgy is not feel-good therapy to cheer people up after a real downer. Certainly liturgy can be a significant way of enabling persons to unite their struggle and grief with the community's, and it can help them to cope with loss. But this is not the time for pious platitudes that "there's a purpose" or naïve assertions that "this is going to make us better." Leaning into lament means being able to make room for protest and complaint. It helps people to share their pain and grief together. It helps them to do so not in despair, but by summoning God and seeking comfort in the hope of things assured (cf. Heb 11:1).

Making a prophetic and ethical commitment

Liturgy in time of disaster has the potential to move us forward and outward and to strengthen in us a resolve to care for the needy, to be mindful of the earth, and to commit ourselves to justice. The "words of our lips and meditation of our heart" (Psalm 19:14) would ring false without a reciprocal commitment of time and resources. This is especially the case for communities that are removed from the event: Liturgy is not there to assuage our "feeling bad" for those poor people; rather, it should help us to name God out of the experience of loss and connect our personal story to the story of God's reign, made known to us in Christ Jesus. Out of the vision of this reign that the liturgy embodies, we are moved to lift up the lowly, to speak a word of peace in the midst of turmoil, to hold the ways of the world accountable to the Gospel.

Our celebration of liturgy in time of disaster and afterward entails responsibility to the other. We need to find ways to remember and to foster the solidarity of living and dead in the great communion with the Crucified One. Liberation theologians like Jon Sobrino and the late Ignacio Ellacuría spoke of the "crucified people," the millions acquainted with suffering, living in abject poverty, held of no account, and innocent without any possibility of avoiding the death that comes in famine or flood or other natural disaster. Liturgy in the wake of disaster should help to foster this communion so that none are forgotten. It should bolster in us the courage to confront that suffering as well. It might also make us vigilant when disaster is caused as much by human hands as it is by the fury of nature.

Liturgy in Time of Natural Disaster
A Model

The following model is offered more to guide local wisdom and imagination than to be a formal script. This outline can serve both for a liturgy in time of immediate response and for a liturgy in solidarity with those who have suffered. This is an example of creative adapting and blending: its inspirations include the old Roman Ritual (*Rituale Romanum*), the Church of England's *Common Worship* ("Facing Pain: A Service of Lament"), the Center for Contemplation and Actions's "Liturgy of Lament Template," and J. Frank Henderson's *Liturgies of Lament*. Any direct borrowing is noted. This order can be celebrated at one time or spread out over a day. It can also be accommodated to a small or large group setting.

The space should be prepared with care. If possible, allow options for people to assume different postures, with open space for sitting on the floor, prostrating, and kneeling; also provide cushions, chairs, or pews. A central focal space could include the bare altar or cross with candles. Provide adequate but dim lighting, especially if it is evening and candles are used. There may be a table or stand for local symbols to be situated near the focal space—around but not on the altar if there is one. An atmosphere of calm and quiet should be fostered, perhaps best evoked with silence rather than any instrumental music. The leader and other ministers, such as a lector or cantor, should join with the assembly in this gathering. Provision should be made for people to help those who are overcome with tears or grief, and perhaps have a counselor available.

Opening

Leader:	God, why have you forsaken us?
	Why are you so far from helping us,
	from the words of our groaning?
	God, come to our assistance!
All:	God, make haste to help us!
Leader:	God, heed our prayers!
All:	God, listen to our cries!

Opening Chant

> *You might consider an ostinato chant or canon like the traditional Hebrew song "Hashiveinu" ("Restore Us to Yourself") or a plaintive Taizé chant or a short song from the Iona Community. The chant would continue for some time to gather the assembly and guide them to a meditative mode.*

Sharing Our Lament

Psalm 102: 1–14

> *You may want to sing the psalm. You can include an antiphon at the beginning and end.*

Silence

Testimony

> *The leader might then invite those who have been affected to share their experiences if they want, or invite all to sit with the pain of the community. As an alternative, an account of the events from the newspaper or an e-mail from someone immediately involved could shape the testimony. The leader concludes the testimony with the follow responsive prayer:*

Responsive Prayer (adapted from *Common Worship*)

Leader: We bring before you, God,
             our confusion in the face of shock,
             our despair in the face of tragedy,
             our helplessness in the face of death.

All: Arise, O God, and come to help us!

Leader: We bring before you, God,
             our tears of sorrow,
             our cries for help,
             our vulnerability of pain.

All: Arise, O God, and come to help us!

Ritual Act

> *This could take the form of processing with the local symbols to the focal space, passing ash or dust to mark oneself or one's neighbor, pouring water or dirt on the ground, extinguishing candles, placing pictures or other objects about the cross, or inviting people to come forward to interact with a natural symbol as they*

are so moved. The focal space could also be where people may assume a posture of prayer—kneeling, prostrating, sitting, or moving to an icon or statue of a saint. Instrumental music or silence is one option, a chant from Taizé or a hymn is another, especially one that expresses grief and lament. The collection of hymns available from the United Methodist General Board of Discipleship "Worship Resources for Times of Crisis" (http:// www.gbod.org/worship/) is a good resource as most printed hymnals lack the repertoire (see C. W. Gillette's "God of Creation" or A. Pratt's "We Once Acclaimed Your Name as 'Love.'" Another resource is the section on "Grief, Fear and Abandonment" in John Bell and the Iona Community's The Last Journey. *The hymn could be sung without an accompanying ritual act or it can conclude the ritual act.*

Confession of Trust in God

Psalm 27

> *You may want to sing the psalm. You can include an antiphon at the beginning and end.*

Silence

Reflection

> *This may take the shape of liturgical preaching, testimony of trust and confidence in God, or an instrumental selection or hymn.*

Responsive Prayer

Leader: God, you have been for us
        shelter and shade,
        steady hand and sure path,
        light and life!

All: We place our trust in you, be with us now!

Leader: God, you have been for us
        safe harbor and refuge,
        hope and peace, mercy and consolation,
        our strength and our salvation!

All: We place our trust in you, be with us now!

> *Some particular mention of God's action related to the natural event might be included.*

Ritual Act

> *This could take the form of anointing with oil, signing/laying on of hands, sprinkling, lighting candles, venerating the cross. During this time, an appropriate hymn or chant may be sung, one that expresses quiet confidence and trust in God.*

Petition for Help

Litany

> *This can take the shape of composed and spontaneous bidding prayers like the prayer of the faithful with the response "Kyrie eleison" or "Lord, hear our prayer." Or it might be a litany of the saints with short petitions added, with a response like "Deliver us, O God" or "Lift us from our burden." Either version should end with the naming of dead, either read from a list or invited to be named spontaneously from the assembly. Incense might be burned through the singing or chanting of the litany. If the situation warrants, it might include a procession from the worship space to the afflicted area and back. In this case, the litany of the saints to start and end the procession would be well suited. The litany's repeated response could be "Kyrie eleison" or "Holy God, Holy and Strong, Holy and Immortal, have mercy on us" (this prayer is known as the Trisagion). When the intercessions are completed (and all are back in the worship space), the leader intones the Lord's Prayer.*

Lord's Prayer

> *The Lord's Prayer concludes the intercessions.*

Words of Assurance and Hope

Reading 1: Romans 8:38–39

Responsory

> Lord, by your cross and resurrection, you have set us free. You are the savior of the world. *(Repeat twice or more.)*

Reading 2: Matthew 11:29–30

Responsory

> Lord, by your cross and resurrection, you have set us free. You are the savior of the world. *(Repeat twice or more.)*

Concluding Collect

Leader: Let us pray. *(Pause for silence.)*
Out of the depths we cry to you, O God!
Our tongues stammer and our words fail
as we behold the disaster that has befallen us.
We wonder: Why, O God?

Though earth and sea may pass away,
your love endures,
and you forget not the people
you have created.

Wipe the tears from our eyes
and support us with your steady arm
in this time of need.

You answered your Son's cry on the cross
by breathing out the Spirit of life and
raising him from death.

Graciously send your Spirit once more
to kindle in us hope and perseverance for the
days ahead
and to keep us in communion with you
and all our beloved dead.

Through Jesus Christ our Savior,
who lives and reigns with you
in the unity of the Holy Spirit,
God, forever and ever.

All: Amen.

Moving to the Future

Charge to the People

Leader: Assured by God's abiding love and comfort
that we do not bear our burdens alone,
let us be ready to ease the burdens of others:
Take a word of hope to the despairing.
Be Christ's hands to build shelter for the homeless.

> Give of what you have been given to those who
> have lost all.
> Support the weak, comfort the mourning,
> and remember the dead.
> *A collection of money or goods for relief services is taken if*
> *appropriate.*

Blessing
Leader: Let us bow our heads to the Lord.
               (Pause for silence.)
               May the peace of God, which is beyond all
               understanding,
               help us persevere with hope and endure the loss.
All: Amen!
Leader: May the love of Jesus Christ, who wept at his
               friend's grave,
               bring us comfort and courage in this time of grief.
All: Amen!
Leader: May the Holy Spirit, who helps us in our weakness
               to pray as we ought,
               be our helper and guide, our true solace and joy.
All: Amen!
Dismissal
Leader: Let us go forth supported by God's hand
               to help our wounded world.
               And as we go, let us be at peace with one another.
Greeting of Peace
      All exchange a sign of peace as they go forth.

Questions for Reflection

1. What are some examples of ritual observances, symbols, and gestures that you have seen or experienced in a time of natural disaster?
2. How does allowing a place for lament in liturgy expand our understanding of who God is for us? Of what liturgy is about?
3. Compose your own prayer or poem to be read at a memorial service for a recent natural disaster. *Or* imagine that you have been asked to

choose the hymns to be sung at such a service. Which three or four hymns would you choose?

Further Reading

Brown, Sally, and Patrick Miller, ed. *Lament: Reclaiming Practices in Pulpit, Pew, and Public Square.* Louisville, KY: Westminster John Knox Press, 2005.

Brueggemann, Walter. "The Costly Loss of Lament." *Journal for the Study of the Old Testament* 36 (1986): 57–71.

Brueggemann, Walter. "Necessary Conditions of a Good Loud Lament." *Horizons in Biblical Theology* 25 (2003): 19–49.

Henderson, J. Frank. *Liturgies of Lament.* Chicago, IL: Liturgy Training Publications, 1994.

Post, Paul, et al. *Disaster Ritual: Explorations of an Emerging Ritual Repertoire.* Liturgia Condenda 15. Leuven: Peeters, 2003.

Power, David. *Worship: Culture and Theology.* Washington, DC: Pastoral Press, 1990. See especially "When Worship Is to Lament," 155–73.

Power, David, and Kabasele Lumbala, eds. *The Spectre of Mass Death.* Concilium 1993/3. London and Maryknoll, NY: SCM Press and Orbis, 1993.

6

Preaching in the Face of Natural Disasters

James A. Wallace, CSsR

The World as a "Vale of Tears"

As a boy, I remember saying prayers that spoke of the world as a "vale of tears." This occurred mostly during novenas, which were part of my Catholic childhood growing up in the 1950s. I can't say that I really thought much about the words at the time. It was one of those phrases that you trusted bore the wisdom of your elders. However, ever since the new millennium began, a case can be made for this designation. From the horror of 9/11 to the bombings—suicide and otherwise—in Iraq that are part of the daily war reports; to the recurring and ongoing examples of genocide in Africa; to the murderous rage of radical groups throughout the world: this precious earth can frequently be viewed through eyes overflowing with tears, if not for one's own lot in life, then certainly for a large portion of the world's population. But the source of such tears is not only due to the evil dwelling in the human heart; our cries also come from events attributed to Mother Nature, or, more ominously, designated as "acts of God."

From the end of December 2004 until mid-October 2005, our world saw an unprecedented number of natural disasters. The tsunami of December 26 in Asia took over 150,000 lives, bringing wholesale destruction to entire villages and towns; in August of 2005 Hurricane Katrina brought massive destruction to Louisiana, Mississippi, and Alabama and death to almost 1,500 people; the October earthquake in Kashmir, Pakistan, claimed 50,000 lives; and mudslides took 1,500 in Guatemala and other countries in Central America around the same time. The immensity of such events challenges our sense of the world as a place of God's gracious presence and protection.

Even tragedies of a lesser magnitude, relatively speaking, leave us struggling for comprehension. In late fall, a man survived a tornado that swept through Evansville, Indiana, in the early hours of the morning with no warning. He told a reporter that a young couple who lived right across the road—with the wife pregnant and a four-year-old son— "should have lived. They had a life in front of them." No matter the size of the catastrophe, the number of dead, the devastation left behind, such events leave people searching to make sense of them in some way. Usually this involves bringing God into the picture, if only to say, "Only God knows why this happened."

This is a long-standing tradition, of course. We even have settled for calling such horrific events "acts of God." Perhaps there is some kind of comfort to think that from some perspective, if only the divine one, these things "make sense." We can even see this interpretation coming into play before the event. As Hurricane Rita was approaching the Texas Gulf Coast less than a month after Hurricane Katrina, the mayor of Port Arthur was interviewed by ABC's Charles Gibson. After being asked whether he was a religious man, the mayor said, "Yes, I am. The Lord is going to do what the Lord's going do. And if he hits us, it's for a reason." And a woman resignedly said, "What are we going to do? God's going to get you whenever he wants."

Even months after these disasters, interpretations continue to be offered, sometimes even contradictory ones. Almost a year later, the *New York Times Magazine* carried an article on several of the tsunami survivors. The author stated that, while one often hears the interpretation that God spared those who were living good lives, others thought that those who had died were the blessed ones because God had removed them from this world of sorrow, this vale of tears, whereas the true sinners were those left behind and given the time to atone for their failures.

Sunday after the Disaster

Such events are certainly on people's minds when they come to church the Sunday after. The questions recur again and again. Why did this happen to me, to us, to them? Why would God allow so many innocent people to lose their lives? And as preachers approach the pulpit, there is the weight of anticipation that spoken words might help. But what light can preachers bring to such occasions? Is there anything that can really be said that will ease the burden at a time of such great loss? Should we simply stand in silence before such awesome events, possibly contributing more by a respectful silence in the face of such loss than by adding to the noise of shallow commentary and ineffectual biblical interpretation?

In the face of these more recent tragic events, there is a new tone of humility evident. Even some of those who usually speak quite assertively about what God has in mind have adopted a more tentative response. In his newsletter *Falwell Confidential*, Jerry Falwell wrote: "What is the biblical significance of all these global disasters which have befallen us recently? The honest answer is, I do not know." This was in marked contrast to Falwell's less-hesitant interpretation of 9/11 as divine judgment for "throwing God out of the public square." In a similar vein of humility, Baptist preacher Randall O'Brien, while recognizing that the Bible itself portrays natural disasters as signs of God's judgment, refrained from preaching this, saying, "I don't know why bad things happen to innocent people. There's something very worshipful about saying that God is God, and I'm not" (see *The Washington Post*, Nov. 5, 2005, B 11). Even so, and granted that there are good grounds to be less certain in reading the divine mind, does silence suffice? Or might the scriptures assist preachers in pondering these events?

The Bible and Preaching

We are reminded in 2 Timothy that we have been sent to "proclaim the message; be persistent whether the time is favorable or unfavorable; convince, rebuke, and encourage, with the utmost patience in teaching" (2 Tim 4:2). The words of the epistle encourage preachers not to sink into silence but to continue to preach the Word—to preach a Word of God that gives life even at a time when death seems everywhere. To repeat, Timothy's letter calls for preachers to "convince, rebuke, and encourage, with the utmost patience in teaching." What needs to be corrected, reproved, appealed to, at this time? What teaching needs to take place to help people survive in spirit and endure the days following these events?

Old Testament scholar Walter Brueggemann offered some helpful thoughts on what it means to take "a biblical view of a natural disaster" in an essay he wrote shortly after the devastating hurricanes in late summer of 2005 (see *The Christian Century*, October 4, 2005, 23). He saw four themes or perspectives that preachers could possibly turn to when viewing these catastrophes in what he called "genuinely biblical terms." In the first perspective, there is the prophetic tradition that clearly links disasters with moral failure. Brueggemann turns our attention to Jeremiah 4:22–27a as providing the clearest instance of this, in which God is portrayed as undoing creation as a response to the evil of God's children. Add God's claim, found in the words of the prophet Isaiah, to "form light and create darkness,…make weal and create woe" (Isa 45:7), and you reinforce the image of God as the source of disasters that bring on darkness and destruction.

While many people might not be sufficiently conversant with the prophets Jeremiah or Isaiah to have picked up on this link between natural disaster and moral failure, a more likely source for such an approach could be found in certain stories in the Old Testament, especially the account of Noah and the flood. At the beginning of this story God is so disgusted with humankind and all of creation that he intends to "blot out from the earth the human beings I have created—people together with animals and creeping things and birds of the air, for I am sorry that I have made them" (Gen 6:7). God is also portrayed as working through the forces of nature, not only in major historical events, such as liberating Israel under Moses by drowning the Egyptians in the sea (Exod 14:26–28), but also on more intimate and fanciful occasions, such as sending both a storm and a very large fish to bring Jonah in line when he was trying to escape God (chapter 1).

Whether these narratives are fact or fiction, they convey the impression that anything that happens in nature is to be laid at the feet of the One who created it. And this even carries over into the New Testament's portrayal of Jesus calming the sea and having the wind and the waves listen to him (Mark 4:35–41) and the Holy Spirit coming under the cover of a strong, driving wind and tongues as of fire that came to rest on those gathered in the upper room (Acts 2:1–4). Given the weight of this biblical imagery and the logical conclusion to be drawn from it, would not this perspective be likely to come to mind for application on most occasions? Even so, are those who suffer most from these disasters, the poor and the already oppressed, to be seen as victims deserving of divine wrath? And can this view be reconciled with the equally logical option for the poor that is the mind of the Creator?

A second perspective Brueggemann finds in the Bible sees the Creator as still engaged in the work of creation, still in the process of bringing order out of chaos. In this perspective, our God is not the omnipotent God we like to think of, but One who can be at the mercy of chaotic forces within creation. Brueggemann refers to Isaiah 51:9–11 as an instance of this, with God being summoned to turn back the chaos, which apparently God has not been able to control. The idea of God as impotent is not a particularly attractive one, yet it may match people's experience at a first stage of movement toward hope. More will be said about this later.

Brueggemann finds a third perspective that puts God's workings at these times of disaster as being beyond our understanding. Such is found at the conclusion of the book of Job (Job 38—41), when God finally speaks out of the storm with a not very consoling response to Job's complaints: "Who are you to question me?" In short, God is God and we are not. We can only stand before the power of nature in wonder and awe, but will be given no satisfying "answers" as to why God is doing all this. The eminent preacher Barbara Brown Taylor strikes a similar note when she writes about certain biblical "texts of terror," whose purpose is "to pry our fingers away from our own ideas about who God is and how God should act, so that there are only two things left to do without fear: use it to propel us toward God who is or let it sink us like a stone." Even so, she concludes that "the hope is that God may yet be present in them, working redemption in ways we are not equipped to discern."

A fourth perspective that Brueggemann finds also brings us to assert that, no matter what, God remains the Lord of creation, and we in faith profess that God is *for* us, and that all will be well. The storm will pass. God will place a rainbow in the sky. Life will once more flourish. Here God has our good at heart and will keep us in the divine care. And while Brueggemann himself does not turn to the New Testament in his article, this would seem to be the basis for the perspective taken there. In the resurrection of Jesus from the dead, we have the preeminent witness to the redemptive will of God. Jesus experienced the power of death and evil in his own body. He was crushed under the weight of the state's injustice and the religious authorities' abuse of power. But, though he was subjected to a most cruel death, he was raised from the dead and made the source of our salvation. In him we find grounds for faith in God's ongoing plan for us and for hope that the age to come is not an illusion but a certainty to be grasped through the eyes of faith.

There are no easy answers, no facile solutions as to what to say after a natural disaster. But as Brueggemann points out, the Bible offers four perspectives, at least, for us to ponder in our search for meaning in the aftermath of a natural disaster: a link with our behavior, or with the yet-to-be conquered power of chaos, or with God's wisdom that stretches beyond our understanding, or with God's ever-faithful commitment to preserve and care for us, no matter what has happened or will befall us. Hopefully, wisdom will guide our choice of perspective when we preach. But preaching itself also offers some guidance at these times when we consider its traditional roles in the life of the believing community, not to be excluded when that community is a suffering one.

The Traditional Tasks of Preaching

Since the beginning of Christianity, preaching has focused on certain fundamental tasks. In *A History of Preaching*, O. C. Edwards notes that preaching's primary work has been in three areas: evangelization, catechesis, and worship. Preaching within evangelization is dedicated to announcing and then helping to bring about the kingdom of God. It is crucial to bringing about an initial response of faith, as Paul reminds us in the Letter to the Romans: "And how are they to believe in one of whom they have never heard? And how are they to hear without someone to proclaim him?" (10:14b–c).

Preaching within catechesis continues the work begun in evangelization and is responsible in most lives for the ongoing deepening of faith. Catechesis is that echoing of the initial message in greater depth and marked by a necessary relevance to life in the world. It includes the teaching of doctrine and provides moral guidance so that believers attain an understanding of what it means to belong to Christ and to live in the power of the Spirit as adopted children of God.

Preaching within worship leads the community to celebrate the paschal mystery in the act of Eucharist, or to participate in the other sacramental rites of baptism, confirmation, reconciliation, anointing, marriage, or orders, all of which deepen our participation in the dying and rising of Christ. Preaching within worship evokes the faith into which we were baptized, eliciting a response of praise and thanksgiving to the living God. Finally, preaching within worship speaks to the hearts and minds of the graced community, enabling it to remember the saving acts of God in the past, to dwell consciously in the presence of God here and now, and to live in hope of a future when all God's promises will be fulfilled. Within the liturgical setting, preaching is meant to fan into flame the faith of the church, even when it has been reduced to embers by life's sorrows, so that the Body of Christ will go forth from the place of gathering into the world with a renewed sense of mission.

All Christian preaching is rooted in the Word of God found in the Bible, the Word given for our instruction. The purpose of this preaching remains what it has always been: to achieve the end for which God sent it into the world. The words of the prophet Isaiah remind us of the promise that accompanies our preaching when God says:

> For as the rain and snow come down from heaven,
>> and do not return there until they have watered
>>> the earth,
>> making it bring forth and sprout,
>>> giving seed to the sower and bread to the eater,
>> so shall my word be that goes out from my mouth;
>>> it shall not return to me empty,
>> but it shall accomplish that which I purpose,
>>> and succeed in the thing for which I sent it.
>>>> (Isa 55:10–11)

This divine intention is at work in our world, even when the rains and winds, earth and sea reveal a more destructive face. As the experience of Elijah on Mount Horeb reminds us, God does not always make his appearance in the earthquake or the heavy wind or the fire (1 Kgs 19:11–13). For whatever reasons, these elements of creation sometimes work according to their own nature, and, perhaps now, this is more likely than ever, due to conditions we have helped create through our own failures to be responsible caretakers of this planet. And where is God in all this? As with Elijah, God waits to speak to us in tiny whispering sounds or even the sound of silence.

For it is when the world has had its life crushed or drowned or broken or torn apart by the forces of nature that it is most in need of a life-giving and faith-sustaining word. More than ever is preaching needed as the waters threaten to overwhelm our bodies and spirits and drag us under, as the earth opens up and swallows our homes and communities, or as the sky sends its terrifying hurricanes and cyclones to wreak destruction and death. The tasks of evangelizing, catechizing, and worshipping are the constant ways of bringing the awareness of the presence of God, and continue to have those roles even in times of disaster. Yet there are also other needs that preaching can address at these times. To these we now turn our attention.

Preaching's Special Role in the Aftermath of a Natural Disaster

Preaching as Weeping

Preaching can play a part in helping a community move from the sorrow, grief, and rage that often accompanies a natural disaster to a place where hope can be reborn. But it is not sufficient to begin where we think people of faith "should" be. All "shoulds" bow to what dwells in the hearts of people who have just suffered nature's blows. While there will come a time to hear once again the good news that the gospel offers, "whether in or out of season," the time may not be right now. The book of Ecclesiastes reminds us:

> For everything there is a season, and a time for every
> matter under heaven:
> a time to be born, and a time to die;
> a time to plant, and a time to pluck up what is planted;
> a time to kill, and a time to heal;
> a time to break down, and a time to build up;
> a time to weep, and a time to laugh;
> a time to mourn, and a time to dance. (Eccl 3:1–4)

These experiences of natural disasters occur in time. And when they occur, God's word reminds us that there is a time to weep and mourn and cry out and lament.

On such occasions, preaching might first attempt to create a space where people can express their loss. In *Preaching as Weeping, Confession, and Resistance*, Christine M. Smith reflects on preaching's capacity to address people after experiences of violence and oppression. The author's focus is on the presence of radical evil in the world, experienced as sexism, racism, classism, and various other forms of oppression, all of which are brought about by human agents. Smith calls preachers to recognize the need of those who suffer such injustices to weep and lament. Certainly this need to weep is present at times of natural disasters. Our preaching may also need to recognize explicitly our inability to give "reasons" for such natural events and especially why the innocent are often the ones to suffer most. Out of the darkness, preaching calls to listeners to resist despair.

Many preachers have moved away from glib assessments and facile interpretations of why natural disasters happen. They no longer link such occurrences with whatever ranks highest on their personal list of societal sins and no longer interpret these events of nature as divine wake-up calls. But blame must not be replaced with silence in the face of these events. While we can't explain them, we can begin a process of helping people move out of their sorrow and loss by offering them a way to express it. Turning to certain psalms of lament can be particularly helpful in this regard. Consider Psalm 69, which begins

> Save me, O God,
>> for the waters have come up to my neck.
> I sink in deep mire,
>> where there is no foothold;
> I have come into deep waters,
>> and the flood sweeps over me.
> I am weary with my crying;
>> my throat is parched.
> My eyes grow dim
>> with waiting for my God. (vv. 1–3)

By the end of this psalm, the speaker has moved to a profession of hope in God and trust in God's care for his people, but the psalmist *starts* his prayer where people often are at times of disaster—in a state of desperation and weariness.

Preaching as Offering Light in the Darkness

While lamenting is often the necessary starting point, there comes a time to move beyond it. Not too long ago a dear friend was diagnosed with inoperable brain tumors. When the word came from the doctors that no operation would be able to remove them, she was with her husband and one of her oldest friends. She sat there in silence, while they wept. But, after a while, she looked at them and said gently but firmly, "That's enough of that now. That will do." There is a time to weep and there is a time to move on.

What helps a person to move on? In *Crisis Preaching: Personal and Public*, homiletician Joseph R. Jeter, Jr., states that "part of the homiletical task is the slow painstaking development of faith that will stand when the storms come" (22), and that this must be done both before and after the crisis. For this reason the preacher must preach in preparation for crisis as well as after it. Regarding the preparatory phase, Jeter makes a play on the word *preaching*, noting that it has a *pre-aching* or *pre-tribulation* function; it plants the seeds that will grow into a sheltering tree when the storm comes. And, of course, preaching has a reconstructive function after the crisis, rebuilding what has been weakened and even partially destroyed.

Particularly helpful are Jeter's suggestions that what needs to be preached in both instances is a message of remembrance, presence, and promise. Preaching can help others to live by remembering what God has done in the past, trusting that God is with us now in the present, and living in a hope rooted in God's promise to be faithful in the future. To this end the images and stories of the Bible continue to hold us up during these times and lead us through the darkness. Such images would include God leading Israel through the desert as a cloud by day and a pillar of fire by night (Exod 13:21); God as the shepherd who leads us through the valley of the shadow of death (Ps 23); God who brings dry bones to life through the power of the prophetic word (Ezek 37:1–14). Especially consoling—

and challenging—is the image of Jesus on the cross at Calvary, surrendering in trust with the words, "Father, into your hands I commend my spirit" (Luke 23:46). This last image cannot be separated from the Easter witness found in all four Gospels that God has raised Jesus from the dead, making him "the first fruits of those who have died" (1 Cor 15:20).

Preaching as Evoking Response

As with all other crisis preaching, preaching in the aftermath of a disaster eventually leads to a call for some kind of response from those not affected. The most immediate response involves doing what we can to assist those who have suffered most. Usually this needs little prompting when the tragedy is close at hand or has come in a dramatic form, although the lesson of both the tsunami of 2004 and Hurricane Katrina of 2005 revealed that even with good will and generous response on the part of people, assistance can be maddeningly inefficient. A year after the tsunami, many of the communities in Southeast Asia were still struggling due to the difficulties of coordinating relief efforts. And a year after the hurricanes in the United States, the signs of wholesale destruction abounded and people remained dislocated.

Part of our response to any natural disaster should be the need to examine ourselves on the role human neglect and/or activity have played in bringing such occurrences about. The conditions that help facilitate the occurrence of natural disasters continue to this day, rooted in our careless stewardship of the environment, whether manifested in our neglect and indifference or in human greed and vested interests. Preaching can call for a more honest appraisal of what we do and what we fail to do on both the macro- and the microlevels of our lives that impact the environment. This will include not only an individual examination of conscience, but also an evaluation of what we do as families, churches, nations, and a world community that can help create the conditions leading to hurricanes and other natural occurrences of such ferocity. Before it is too late, steps must be taken not only by government and business leadership, but by all of us, to look to the protection and conservation of our vital resources: the air, water, and ecosystems on which all life depends. Preaching needs to address such matters, and the hour to do this is sooner rather than later.

In summary, the three goals of preaching at times of natural calamities—moving a community to lament, to profess faith in God, and to resolve to act in response—also offer preachers an appropriate structure. Grieving our loss is the starting point, giving way to a call to remembering what God has done and has promised to do, and calling for a response to this God by taking up God's work of bringing relief to those who have suffered. Such a threefold movement could take place during a single preaching event or it might be spread out over a period of time. In the end our preaching calls people to turn to faith in the God of Jesus Christ in whom they have been baptized and to draw on that faith in order to live in hope. The God of Israel and Father of our Lord Jesus Christ does not abandon us nor fail to keep his promises.

A Homily in the Aftermath of the Tsunami

The following is an example of a homily preached a few days after the tsunami of December 2004. The occasion was the feast of the Epiphany. An effort was made to recognize the horror of the event, to address how people were interpreting it, and to bring this tragic occurrence into dialogue with a proclamation of the feast that is the crown of the Christmas season with its core message of incarnation and what it means for the world.

The Epiphany of the Lord

Was *That* an Epiphany? Was *That* a Manifestation of God?

We have been overwhelmed in recent days with images of the tsunami and its legacy of death and destruction. It has been a week of death on a scale that is incomprehensible, too much for us to grasp. One hundred and twenty thousand reported dead so far. This horrific event has led some to raise questions.

"Is this a punishment of Allah or a test?" asked Islam Online.

Others were more definite: "This is an expression of God's great anger with the world," said Israel's Sephardic Chief Rabbi. And another Jewish leader's voice was raised in a similar vein: "The world is being punished for wrongdoing, for people's hatred of each other, lack of charity, moral turpitude."

A Hindu leader was quoted as saying, "The tsunami is divine retribution."

A particularly outrageous reaction came from a Christian leader who thought the miraculous survival of many Christians in countries where Christianity is greatly persecuted, such as Sri Lanka, India, and Indonesia, was a sign of where God stood.

But this last comment was balanced by theologian Martin Marty who noted, "People are asking for trouble when they are precise in knowing God's will."

I agree with Dr. Marty, yet would qualify his statement in light of today's feast.

Today we have a feast that features an epiphany of nature, a star leading a band of astrologers to the place where the infant God-human lies. It is a feast that continues the Christmas proclamation that our God is Emmanuel, God-with-us; a feast that offers a certain precise understanding of God's will: to be with us.

Many might be tempted to respond, "Really? God with us? All the time? Day and night? Well, where was God as the tsunami slammed into the homes of some of the poorest people in our world? Where was God-with-us as men, women, and children were carried off by the water?"

One must be very careful when one claims to offer God's perspective on any event. Even so, I really do not think God stirs up tsunamis or earthquakes or hurricanes or floods, or any other such disasters, to punish people. If the Christmas season proclaims anything, it is that God is irrevocably *for* us, hence, the name Emmanuel—God-with-us.

Our God is a God of the journey—from the beginning when God sent Abram and Sarai forth from Haran. God was with Jacob when he set off, fleeing his brother Esau's murderous threats. God was with Joseph when his brothers threw him into the pit, and when he found himself imprisoned down in Egypt because of the false accusations of Potiphar's wife. And God was with Moses and the people as they set out from their land of slavery to find a place where they could live in peace, and worship the God who had claimed them as his own.

Today's story is, in the end, a story about the journey we all make to arrive at the place where we find God. Matthew's story tells us about some astrologers who picked up on the signs that were around them, and got to the right place by staying attentive to the world about them. The lesson we might hear from this text is that God instructs us from the "stuff" of our lives, from the everyday moments, the events that befall us, the joys and sorrows we experience. More specifically, God is with us in all that happens. God does not abandon us.

The real light God has set before us is the light that comes from the vision our faith gives. Paul speaks of the light of the revelation he received: the vision of Gentiles and Jews as children of the same God, coheirs and copartners, members of the same body. It is this vision that allows us to continue to "rise up in splendor" and to reflect the light that has shone on us, the glory of the Lord that is the grace of Jesus Christ within us.

We often lose sight of that light. Indeed, we often are the cause of deep darkness.

I saw the movie *Hotel Rwanda* last night. It dramatizes the efforts of one man to be a light in the world, and to save some of the Hutus who were being slaughtered by the Tutsis. It is a story of deep sadness: 800,000 people were slaughtered. And the world watched and did nothing—including us.

We did nothing.

As horrific as this tsunami has been for all those it touched, the response of people around the world has been its own sign. We are truly brothers and sisters bound together by a common humanity.

We continue to walk, often through darkness, but nevertheless we are assured that, at the end, we will arrive where God dwells. The journey of the Magi is the one we take every week when we come here. Like the Magi, we arrive at a place where we can learn more about the God we seek. Like the Magi who came to Jerusalem where the words of the prophets were consulted, we come here to hear the words of prophets, apostles, and evangelists. Like the Magi, we finally arrive at the place where the Lord is to be found—in the sacrament of his body and blood.

God continues to draw us onto the road, out into the places where it is not always safe. May we walk the path, through times of darkness and times of emerging light, with hearts of faith, hope, and love for all who are on the road with us. May we be attentive to the signs that are given—those set above our heads and those placed within our hearts. And may we finally come to the place where we can offer our own gifts, especially the one that God cherishes most of all: a heart open to receive the light, a mind able to see the signs, and a spirit willing to do God homage.

A Final Word

The God we know in Jesus Christ is present even in disasters, sharing in our suffering and calling us to become a new creation. I believe God's heart joined in the suffering of the people who died and those who suffered and endured the loss of loved ones and homes during the tsunamis, the hurricanes, the earthquakes, the cyclones and tornados, and the floods of recent years. I believe God's healing presence was at work during these sad times, just as I believe that God's justice will confront those who failed to do all in their power to respond to these victims. I believe that God wishes to open our eyes and ears to the cries for justice and compassion that come from poor and hungry people here and elsewhere; to shake us from our complacency and materialism; and to move us to seize the opportunities we have to foster justice in our nation and in our world; and to assume our rightful responsibility to care for God's creation, so graciously entrusted to us. As preachers, may we find and offer the comfort that God's word brings when the waves sweep over us and the earth shakes beneath our feet, and with that word build a bridge for our people to cross over onto the high ground of faith and hope in God and love for our neighbor in need.

Questions for Reflection

1. What do you think of God when natural disasters occur? What kind of God do you speak of or preach by your words and actions to others when such disasters strike?
2. What do you think is important for preachers to say at a time of natural disaster, and what should they *not* say?
3. What response should preachers ask from those not directly touched by such disasters for those who have been?

Resources

Edwards, O. C., Jr. *A History of Preaching*. Nashville: Abingdon, 2004.

Jeter, Joseph R., Jr. *Crisis Preaching: Personal and Public*. Nashville: Abingdon, 1998.

Smith, Christine M. *Preaching as Weeping, Confession, and Resistance: Radical Responses to Radical Evil*. Louisville: Westminster John Knox Press, 1992.

Taylor, Barbara Brown. "Preaching the Terrors." In *The Art and Craft of Biblical Preaching*, edited by Haddon Robinson and Craig Brian Larson, 623–26. Grand Rapids: Zondervan, 2005.

7

Plague, Famine, Yellow Fever
Religious Repercussions
of Three Natural Disasters
John Vidmar, OP

It is instructive to examine how the Christian Church and average Christians have dealt with natural disasters in its two-thousand-year history. I cannot begin to catalog every natural disaster and the reaction it received, but I would like to focus on three very different episodes in the life of the Church that are instructive, not only about how the official Church responded, but especially about how average Catholics responded. The first, the Black Death (1347–51), was an international catastrophe, in which possibly as many as 75 million people died. The second, the Potato Famine (1847–51), was a national disaster for Ireland. And the third, yellow-fever epidemics in Memphis, Tennessee (1873, 1878, 1879), were a local calamity. In each of these natural disasters, the Catholic Church and individual Christians reached out for God in different ways.

The Black Death, 1347–51

The first episode I would like to treat is the Black Death of the years 1347–51. It was probably the greatest natural disaster, in terms of human lives lost, in the history of the known world. While I do not wish to minimize the catastrophe of a local phenomenon such as Hurricane Katrina, in which well over one thousand people died, it is estimated that as many as 75 *million* people died worldwide from the Black Death in a four-year period. In Europe, where the statistics were better recorded, the death toll was appalling and probably approached 20 million victims.

Contemporaries estimated that one-third of the total population of Europe died in a few short years. More recent studies have increased that percentage to one-half and as high as two-thirds. Whatever the details, the effects of the Black Death were devastating, and helped to change the course of the history of the Church.

It began in Sicily in 1347, where a ship coming from the Middle East brought a contagious disease that experts have since identified as bubonic plague, spread by fleas on rats. The disease attacked the lymph nodes, and got the name "bubonic" from the Greek word for groin, *boubon*, where the lymph nodes were most commonly infected. (The swellings in the lymph nodes were called "buboes.") The skin would darken and often be accompanied by the vomiting of black fluid. Having contracted the disease, a person could die within twenty-four hours or linger for a few days. Large cities were especially vulnerable, having the largest number of rats and the most crowded and unsanitary conditions. In Paris, one-half of the population (fifty thousand people) died, sometimes as high as eight hundred per day. In Florence, one-half of the population died. In Venice, two-thirds of the population died, nearly six hundred per day. England went from having a population of seven million to two million in a few years.

Such devastation took a terrible toll, and not just in human life. The fear that was engendered—as well as the hopelessness of watching one's loved ones and neighbors die regardless of age or sex—was unimaginable. Whenever a cataclysm of this nature takes place, anger and fear need to be directed. *Something, someone*, must be responsible. Since the cause of the Black Death would not be known for several centuries, and since the plague would continue to afflict Europe in lesser episodes for the next few decades, the common person felt the need to assign blame for the catastrophe.* This blame-game went in several directions. Minorities were suspect, as they always are, for somehow bringing about the spread of the disease. Jews were especially suspect since they had a lesser incidence of plague death—probably owing to their ritual cleansing laws and their isolation in ghettos—and they suffered reprisals from the populace as a result. So widespread were these pogroms that the pope

---

*Any communicable disease was known as "the plague," but the bubonic plague seems to have been a frequent visitor.

(Clement VI) issued a bull in 1348 protecting the Jews, in which he pointed out that they were suffering as much as everyone else.

It was more common to blame either the moral state of Europe at the time or, more specifically, the scandalous state of the Church's hierarchy. When the Black Death rampaged through Europe in the late 1340s, the Catholic Church was experiencing the Avignon Papacy, in which the pope had simply moved, for a number of very good reasons, to reside in Avignon under the protection of the French king. However, as it became clear with time that this was not a temporary arrangement, and that the popes might permanently take up residence outside Rome even though they are the bishops of Rome, a certain discontent gripped the Christian world. The Black Death was viewed by some as God's judgment on the situation.

The Church hierarchy does not seem to have responded to this criticism with any urgency. The popes remained in Avignon and, while the Black Death raged, one pope sat in a chair between two large fires, which were kept burning all day, not knowing exactly why such a measure would keep him safe (though uncomfortable). Most bishops seemed at a loss as to what to do or say, and understandably so. The lower clergy and religious responded heroically, for the most part. They were the ones, obviously, who could actually do something to help. Burying the dead and tending to the stricken were two very hazardous jobs indeed, and many clergy and religious died as a result. So great was the loss of life within the ranks of the Church that it has often been pointed to as a remote reason for the Reformation, which would come 150 years later. Morally good, well-educated priests and religious who died caring for the sick would be replaced by people who were not as morally rigorous or as well-educated, and this led to the harsh criticism of the clergy and religious that we find in Erasmus, who wrote just before the Reformation. But the Church's record, in terms of its reaction to the Black Death, is one of which it can be very proud.

But what was not foreseen was the reaction of the average Christian, which moved in several directions. One direction was to despair of moral life altogether and to fall into the attitude of "eat, drink, and be merry—for tomorrow you die." Even the children's game "Ring around the rosey" has a certain fatalism to it. We dance around a bush with our "pocket full of posey," a bag of herbs tied around the neck, but we "all fall dead" anyway. Boccacio's *Decameron*, written at this time, features the telling of mostly bawdy stories by seven women and three men who have fled from the Black Death in Florence. Their point is that the new, emerging mercantile class, with its worldly and cynical wisdom, is a far better and more realistic world than that of monks and the Church.

The opposite extreme saw the appearance of *flagellants*, who regarded the Black Death as a judgment by God on a sinful world, and the only way to remove this judgment was to impose physical penances on themselves. There is something of this in Mel Gibson's film *The Passion of the Christ*, in which the scourging scene is carried out in greater length than it needed to be, with the idea that the more Christ *suffered*, the more complete would be our salvation. In any case, the flagellants became a significant movement, and they moved even the common person, who would not join them, to consider doing more on a personal level in terms of prayer and moral behavior.

Thus was born the real historical result of the Black Death, the turning of the average Christian to a more private form of prayer and devotion. This coincided with a movement within the Church to personalize one's faith. The writing of the mystics, especially that of Thomas à Kempis, who wrote the masterpiece *The Imitation of Christ*, emphasized a personal response to the call of the Lord. Churches, for one thing, were looked on as dangerous places to go—any large gathering of people would be avoided as possibly spreading the disease.

Another work of literature, *Piers Plowman* by Thomas Langland, also addressed the Black Death. While it deplored the state of the Church, and especially the hierarchy, it also called on the common Englishman— the "plowman"—to do his job, be honest and hard-working, and say his prayers. Langland challenged common Christians to stop blaming other people for their woes, start living Christian lives themselves, and thereby, hopefully, to change the world for the better.

When the Reformation came, personal religion, rather than communal rituals, were called for. Sacred scripture was to be read and interpreted by everyone individually. The Church fragmented into many parts, and is still fragmenting. In the Protestant world, communal events such as pilgrimages, town plays performed by various guilds, and parish ales (or festivals) often gave way to an austere service of the Word with a demand for individual repentance.

Another effect of the Black Death was to alter the social structure of Europe, which would disturb what had been a threefold balance of power: king, nobility, and Church. Because the nobility and Church had lost so much of their base of loyalty, and because so much farm land was now turned to pasture, the king's power rose, and with it the power of a new mercantile class that was not dependent on either the landed gentry or the Church. Not only would the monasteries find themselves with fewer monks and tenants to farm the land, but they would be looked on as a soft target for princes who were intent on increasing their budgets without taxing their people. Monasteries in England, with their large estates which once held four hundred men, now (in the early 1500s) held forty, and sometimes four. This caught the King of England's acquisitive eye, which was not for monastic land alone. The monasteries also provided the only serious objections to his proposal to divorce his first wife, Catherine of Aragon, marry Ann Boleyn, and declare himself the head of the Church. By dissolving the monasteries, which Henry VIII did in four short years, he managed not only to steal their lands, but silence their opposition. The Black Death, coming as it did 150 years before, and weakening these religious orders, helped him get away with it.

The Irish Potato Famine, 1846–51

Five hundred years later, the second greatest natural (or peacetime) disaster since the Black Death took place in Ireland, beginning in 1847 (some will argue 1846). A blight affected the potato crop. Scholars have identified this as a specific fungus, the exact identity of which has been recently questioned. But whatever the details, almost one million people died in Ireland from starvation or related diseases, while Irish landlords were exporting beef and other foodstuffs. There are all kinds of charges to be meted out: to the landlords who evicted their starving tenants; to the British government, which helped in a very half-hearted and ineffective way; even to upper-class English Catholics, one of whom said, "What can we do for the Irish? We can pray for them." To their credit, a number of English Catholic writers came to the defense of their coreligionists. Hilaire Belloc wrote a particularly powerful essay in defense of the Irish, but, for the most part, financial help came from overseas, especially the United States. The Irish did not need essays; they needed food.

The effect on the Irish was stunning and very different from the reactions to the Black Death. Before the famine, Ireland had long been a country in which practice of the faith had been half-hearted, and Catholicism more a source of national identity than a means of spiritual growth. As late as the early 1840s, Ireland was not a particularly church-going country. This all changed in 1847. The entire country seemed to turn to God to help them in their plight. Vocations to the priesthood and religious life rose and would remain high for 150 years.

The Irish suffered as a nation and directed their common anger toward the English, whose political policies were regarded as allowing the advent of famine, and thus they found themselves strongly united in an extraordinary way. This political unity would fuel the desire for independence, which finally came in 1922. Much as the United States experienced an unusual level of unity during the Great Depression and World War II, the Irish experienced a similar coming-together because of their shared suffering.

Another result of the famine was that the Irish spread throughout the English-speaking world through emigration. Millions of Irish landed on the shores of Canada, the United States, and Australia, and transformed those countries. Not only did big cities—like Boston in the once most-puritanical and anti-Catholic state, Massachusetts—find themselves run by Irish Catholics, but the Catholic Church in the United States suddenly awoke to find itself run by the Irish as well. It was a Catholicism which was not merely political, but one which had become devout. The Holy Name Society, begun by Dominicans in the late 1800s, suddenly spread to every parish in the United States, many of which were Irish. In 1924, after World War I, a huge parade of a hundred thousand Holy Name members marched from the Capitol to the White House, affirming their patriotism to the country. Sixteen thousand of the soldiers killed in World War I were Roman Catholic, and the Holy Name Society wanted to make that better known. The famous Dominican preacher Ignatius Smith ended his oration at Arlington Cemetery with these words:

> And now, we call out to you States and to you represen-
> tatives of the Catholic dioceses of the United States to
> report what our Holy Name Society men did for the
> United States during the World War. Tell us how they
> served and how they died. Tell this unknown Buddy

how they supported him during the War so that he and heaven may know how they are prepared to support him in peace. Let him know and ask his spirit in another world to inform our fellow-citizens that when unstinted service for America is ever demanded whether in war or in peace from American citizens, this service will be found in the ranks of the Holy Name Society represented here in Arlington.

Irish Catholicism had arrived and, even though it would be supported and modified by waves of Catholic immigrants from Eastern Europe and Italy, it was the battering ram that broke down centuries of anti-Catholicism in North America. The first labor union, the Knights of Labor, was headed by an Irish Catholic named Terence Powderly. He was defended in Rome, which was suspicious of secret societies, by an Irish-American, Cardinal Gibbons of Baltimore, who warned the Vatican away from condemning this group by saying he could take care of things.

Common suffering does not necessarily lead to despair. It can be focused toward the good, both through a mutual concern for those who are suffering and an awareness of a greater good than the world we inhabit. I met a middle-aged man a few years ago who said he lived in my old Slovenian neighborhood in Cleveland, and he wanted to know if the butcher shop on East 74th Street was owned by my grandfather. I said it was. He then related how, during the Depression, my grandfather would extend credit to people at no interest and let food bills accumulate. This man ended by saying, "Your grandfather kept the neighborhood fed." A lot of people did that for each other during the Depression, and we can learn from them about how it is done.

The Yellow Fever Epidemics in Memphis, Tennessee, 1873–79: St. Peter's Church

Until the early 1900s, the three "plagues" most common in the United States were cholera, small pox, and yellow fever. Much like the Black Death, these diseases were fearsome because so little was known about them. Yellow fever remained a mystery until Dr. Walter Reed isolated its cause—a virus transmitted by mosquitoes—in 1900. Certain facts were known about it: it usually appeared in the summer and disappeared after the first frost; immigrants from Europe were especially susceptible to it; of those who contracted the disease, the white population suffered a 70 percent fatality rate while the black population's fatality rate was an astonishingly low 7 percent, a fact that caused everyone to wonder if the disease was not a divine comment on the outrage of slavery. Yellow fever was especially virulent in the Southern states, though it was not unknown as far north as Philadelphia and New York. In one hospital alone, Charity Hospital in New Orleans, the average yearly number of deaths from yellow fever was two hundred. By far, the worst epidemics occurred in Philadelphia in 1793, Galveston in 1839, and New Orleans in 1853. In 1867 the fever, sometimes known as "yellowjack," claimed the lives of three thousand people in New Orleans and another thousand in Galveston. But this was nothing compared to what was about to happen in Memphis. In the three years of 1873, 1878, and 1879, Memphis would see the deaths of ten thousand of its inhabitants.

The Dominican parish of St. Peter's would find itself in the center of the maelstrom. Not only were its parishioners affected (four thousand of the dead were Catholic), but the parish also worked with an orphanage run by Dominican sisters. The pastor, Father Joseph Augustine Kelly, OP, lived through all three epidemics and kept a diary that today provides a very valuable record of the heroism shown by the religious and townspeople in the midst of disaster. The diary entry for September 23, 1873, begins with the description of a fund-raising picnic for the orphans and the humorous (to us) mention of a new game called "baseball," which Father Kelly says "will never last as it is very violent." But the next sentences are shocking:

> Fr. Dailey died today of yellow-fever; he was sick less than 48 hours. Got his death in attending sick calls. The disease is mostly in Happy Hollow [an Irish ghetto near the Mississippi River], but is now spreading through the city. I am kept very busy.... One of the Franciscan nuns is dead, another is expected to die. All the sisters are waiting on the sick.

Father Dailey was twenty-seven years old and had been ordained for only eleven months. In less than four weeks Father Kelly recorded that four Dominican priests, three Dominican sisters, and a Franciscan priest were dead. In a few months, two thousand people would join them. Father Kelly himself caught the fever during a double burial and barely survived. But, little did he know it, he was now immune from yellow fever.

Four years of peace ensued, but the fever struck again in August of 1878. Of the city's fifty thousand people, 60 percent (thirty thousand) fled north in understandable panic. The stories of the people who remained are of incredible heroism, and most of these are motivated by a search for God, and a desire to bring God to the afflicted. Members of different religious denominations and even different religions assisted each other, as when an Episcopalian minister stopped some Catholic sisters and gave them fifty dollars to help them in their work. Even more unusual is the story of the only Jewish rabbi in Memphis at the time, who narrated the following tale:

> While passing along Shelby Street...a man called to me for help from the window of a three-story house. "Money or medicine?" I asked as I entered the house; I always carried with me a certain amount of both. "Not food, nor money, nor doctor," the man replied, "nor anything for myself. It is for my wife. She already has the black vomit, the sure sign of death, and we are Catholics, and she wants a priest. Can you get a Catholic priest for her?"
>
> I assured him, and hastened to St. Peter's. I informed the priest [Father Kelly], and accompanied him as he carried the Sacrament with great respect down the forsaken streets of afflicted Memphis. I showed him the house and room, and remained until the father had administered the rites, and then returned with him. Never perhaps in history had the sight been seen before: a Jewish rabbi running for a Catholic priest, and both going side by side along the streets of a desolate city to bring to a dying Catholic the rites of her religion.

Another remarkable instance of cooperation—this time between races—occurs in the person of Sam Henderson, a former slave, who is still known fondly today as "St. Peter's Sam." He began helping at St. Peter's and would remain there for thirty-five years. During the epidemics he was asked not to follow the priests on their sick calls, as this was extremely hazardous duty, but (in his own words) he "stoled after" the priests to make sure they got to their destination and back safely. He also clothed in their habits all of the eight Dominican priests who died from the fever. Such was the gratitude of the Dominican

Sam Henderson,
"St. Peter's Sam"

community that, when Sam Henderson died of natural causes long after the fever days were over, he was buried at a solemn High Mass, and all eight pallbearers were Dominican priests. They bought him a monument for his grave that reads, "Here lie the remains of Samuel Henderson, St. Peter's Sam."

The contribution of the sisters was also enormous. Twenty-three sisters died in the three years of the epidemic. Their sacrifice is exemplified by the fate of five Franciscan sisters who arrived in early September of 1878 as volunteers. By September 12 four of the five were dead. Father Kelly had anointed four Dominican sisters within the same hour on August 25 of the same year.

Cooperation between Dominican men and women can best be seen in their joint running of St. Peter's Orphan Asylum. Father Kelly arranged in 1878, with the assistance of the bishop of Nashville, for all fifty-three orphans to be transported to Nashville. The question of the legality of this action—Memphis was under a strict quarantine—did not deter the Dominican men and women from getting their orphans to safer ground. As soon as they had departed, Father Kelly took in another thirty-two orphans in the old building. In the following year, Father Kelly bought a twenty-five-acre tract of land in the country and moved the orphans and five Dominican sisters there in the hopes of avoiding the fever. That year, while so many were dying in the city, only one of the ninety-six children died of yellow fever.

Father Kelly's first concern had always been for the orphans, whose numbers were large owing to the combination of the recent Civil War and the yellow-fever epidemics. So it is fitting that the last entry in his diary concerned them: "Baptized thirteen orphans this month." At his funeral, the orphans marched down the center aisle of St. Peter's church and placed flowers on his casket as a tribute to their protector, "The Father of the Orphans."

A touching testimony to the work of this pastor was given by one of the young Dominicans who died in Memphis in 1878. Patrick Scannell had arrived at St. Peter's from Louisville, Kentucky, on September 12 and would be dead a week later. But he wrote the following (in pencil) to a friend in the Louisville priory:

> You cannot have any idea about the state of things here, it is…terrible. The streets are deserted, and one finds nobody except a few police patrols. I have not seen five whites since I've been here. Yesterday, Sunday, I said Mass in our church for fifty people. Father Kelly seems well, but tired. He came to me with open arms, and is full of gratitude to the priests of Louisville for their kindness and aid. He is truly a Christian hero. He never mentions a word about his hardships and sufferings. We are always together whenever there is a free moment, and the more I know him the more I love him.

Natural disasters produce heroes, such as Father Kelly and Sam Henderson and those who died tending to the sick and the dying. Adversity also produces more ordinary heroes, such as the parish priest who came to my mother's house, when she was a child during the Depression. He brought clothing and canned food and money, whenever he had it to give, to give to her mother, who was trying to raise six children by herself.

My grandmother, whom I never met and who used to take in laundry and do what she could to raise money to support her family, was a saint. A few years ago, I got a Christmas card from a childhood friend of my mother's, who said that whenever she went to visit, my grandmother would invite her into the house to wait (my mother was late even then).

The friend would sit underneath the ironing board while my grandmother sang songs about the Blessed Mother and the saints. She wrote, "I eventually became a Catholic because of your grandmother and those wonderful days spent underneath the ironing board."

Natural disasters occur. We need to learn from our forebears how to deal with them. May they rest in peace. And may perpetual light shine upon them. And upon us.

Questions for Reflection

1. Would you volunteer to help people in the midst of a natural disaster if it meant exposure to the disease and probable death?
2. What kind of courage can you imagine it takes to do this?
3. Have you experienced a natural disaster, or do you know anyone who has experienced a natural disaster? How has the Church responded? How does the Church respond today?

Bibliography

Black Death

Tuchman, Barbara. *A Distant Mirror: The Calamitous 14th Century.* New York: Knopf, 1978. One chapter concerns the Black Death, situating it in the context of other events of the fourteenth century.

Irish Potato Famine

Donnelly, James S. *The Great Irish Potato Famine.* Thrup, Stroud, Glos., UK: Sutton, 2001.

Yellow Fever in Memphis

Vidmar, OP, John. *Fr. Fenwick's "Little American Province": 200 Years of the Dominican Friars in the United States.* New Hope, KY: New Hope Press, 2005. Available through Dominican Provincial Archives, Providence College, Providence RI 02918.

8

Looking at Nature
"From Both Sides Now"
Nancy de Flon

As you drive north on Interstate 87, which runs between Albany and the Adirondack Mountains of New York, somewhere before exit 30, which leads through the heart of the High Peaks region into Lake Placid, a mountain aptly named Giant of the Valley comes into view. Giant Mountain isn't so much a single peak as it is a huge massive, and the enormity of it as it gradually unfolds on your left is sure to elicit a wide-eyed gasp or two. If you are photographically inclined, you will regret the absence of a lay-by from which to immortalize the awesome sight with your camera, until you realize that no one photograph could do it justice.

Now let the scene shift. You are no longer in your car, watching Giant of the Valley unfold before you from a distance of fifteen miles. Instead you are on top of the mountain. It's a scorchingly hot August day, the sun is relentlessly beating down on you, and you've underestimated the amount of liquid you would need to take along to drink on this day-hike.

You could survive having brought along insufficient food. You could even survive, albeit with considerable discomfort, an onslaught of the ruthlessly persistent blackflies or mosquitoes. But leave those extra bottles of water or Gatorade at home, and you've made a potentially fatal mistake; dehydration will surely kill where starvation and insects fail to do so.*

Giant Mountain as breath-taking scenery and Giant Mountain as potential killer—you've looked at Giant of the Valley "from both sides

---

*My son actually had this experience in August 1996. When he emerged from the trailhead to where I was waiting for him with the car after his eight-mile traverse, he looked as if he had been trekking in Death Valley.

now," as Judy Collins sang in the 1960s. And in reflecting on where we might look for God in natural disasters, one of my favorite places is precisely in nature's "both-sidedness": the fire that can fill our homes with warmth on a chill winter day or reduce them to a heap of cinders; the water that can cleanse us and quench our thirst or devastate and drown; the mountain that can pose majestically for an awesome picture or kill us if we get stuck on it without water on a hot summer day, or lose our way in a winter whiteout.

Let me make it clear: I am not suggesting that nature's Creator is both good and evil; nor am I saying that nature's "both sides" reflect a dualistic situation in which a "good God" is opposed to an equally powerful "Evil One." As Catholics we don't believe these things. What I do want to offer for consideration, however, is that much of the awesome magnificence of nature lies in the variety of its manifestations—even, perhaps, in its unpredictability—and this, in turn, reflects the mystery and unfathomableness of God.

Sources from Antiquity

Whether it functions literally or symbolically, water is the natural element par excellence whose both-sidedness runs like a red thread throughout the Hebrew and Christian Scriptures, as well as through our liturgy. The peoples of the ancient Near East regarded water as a hostile, primeval power. Water and floods represented chaos, an unruly force over which only the most valiant god or hero could prevail. In Babylonian religion, the god Marduk conquered Tiamat, the monster of primeval chaos, and thereby became lord of the gods of heaven and earth. Among the Israelites, of course, it was Yahweh who triumphed over these primitive powers of chaos, a deed celebrated in the poetry of the Hebrew Bible. Psalm 29 describes the Lord sitting enthroned over the flood; Psalm 93 declares that the Lord is more majestic than the thundering waters or the waves of the sea. The splendid canticle of Habbakuk musters every natural image in the prophet's arsenal to depict Yahweh's victory over the primeval elements. Vestiges of Yahweh's mastery over the power of water can be found in a passage from Job, in which God talks about how he has determined the boundaries of the sea: "Hitherto shall you come but no further." On the Thirteenth Sunday in Ordinary Time in Cycle B, our liturgy couples this reading with the gospel story of Jesus calming the storm. Mark's terse account has one objective: to dramatize Jesus' power over the raw, elemental force of nature and, thereby, to demonstrate his divinity. A man who could exert such power was God indeed.

Water's primeval destructive powers can function as metaphor for overwhelming torment and troubles. Who could read the opening lines of Psalm 69, for example—"Save me, O God, / for the waters have come up to my neck.... / I have come into deep waters, / and the flood sweeps over me" (vv. 1, 2b)—without thinking of the victims of the tsunamis in Asia or of Hurricane Katrina?

Yet water also quenches thirst. In Psalm 42, the deer yearning for running streams is a simile for a soul longing for God; in John 4, the Samaritan woman's need for fresh water draws her to the well and to a life-changing encounter with Jesus; and restful waters revive our spirits when, led by the Lord, we sit down by them (Ps 23:2b).

Water's duality figures in the First Letter of Peter: God destroyed the world through the flood and yet God also saved (those on the ark) through the same waters (1 Pet 3:18–22). The same God who destroyed the world with water also gives life through the waters of baptism, for which the living water promised by Jesus to the Samaritan woman is a symbol. And who can claim a more dramatic experience of the "both sides" of water than St. Peter? Peter saw his Lord walk on water. He stepped out and successfully walked on that same stormy sea until he stopped too long to ask himself what on earth he was doing; then he began to sink, until Jesus raised him up.

The biblical poems and stories are only one example of ancient people's views of divine power over nature. From the Israelites' neighbors in the ancient Near East, right up to the myths of the Nordic people of a thousand years ago, nature theophanies developed in an attempt to explain the causes of natural phenomena by peoples who lacked the wherewithal to advance scientific explanations. Ancient peoples readily accepted that their deities were behind the duality of nature: the god who drenched the earth with rain to make plants sprout was the same god who caused rivers to overflow so that crops were ruined and people lost their homes and perhaps their lives. Lacking the knowledge available for scientific explanations, ancient peoples had no need to indulge in theological anguish over why a good god could cause bad things to happen. It is we, in our advanced technological society, who seem cursed with the need to formulate such reasons. For our forebears, including our forebears in the faith, the acceptance of the notion of a god as a direct, primary cause of nature's duality was, well, natural. For us in the twenty-first century, however, such a mindset amounts to a Calvinistic view, for which there is no excuse. But more of that later.

Both-sidedness in the Arts

Numerous members of the Communion of Saints have responded to nature's duality by expressing it in poetry or painting; thus, their artistic legacy is a related place in which to look for God. After the eighteenth and early nineteenth centuries, when poets tended to romanticize nature or to extract from it a moral lesson, there gradually came a shift to incorporating an awareness of nature's destructive potential. This came about when the "grand tour" became fashionable and when the pastime of alpinism developed in popularity, and people could now see and, unfortunately, experience at first hand the "down side" (literally) of previously idealized elements of nature. Mountains were grand to look at and they revealed God's sublimity—but you could also fall off them and be killed. Interestingly, the first incidence of a poet recording such an event occurs not in his verse but in his prose: Samuel Taylor Coleridge's account (in his letter to Sara Hutchinson, 1802) of his foolhardy descent of Sca Fell, in the Lake District of England, is considered the earliest classic of mountaineering literature. That particular route down England's second-highest mountain (3,162 feet) is known as Broad Stand, and present-day guidebooks strongly advise against it.

By the time Gerard Manley Hopkins was penning verses, knowledge of the risks inherent in close engagement with nature was pretty well established. Ironically, it was the Jesuit poet, whose phrase "God's grandeur" has become a byword for the awesome beauty of nature as reflective of its divine spark, who followed in the psalmist's literary footsteps by using the vivid imagery of hurtling headlong down a steep mountainside as a metaphor for descent into depression: "O the mind, mind has mountains; cliffs of fall / Frightful, sheer, no-man-fathomed."

Looking further to the twentieth century, what more dramatic exposition of nature's "both sides" could there be than Benjamin Britten's opera *Peter Grimes,* whose true protagonist is not its eponymous antihero

106

but the sea—now glittering prettily in the morning sun, now dealing devastation during one of those tempests that are the bane of the residents along the East Anglian coast as well as of the ships that ply its waters? (Recall that it wasn't far from here that the wreck of the *M. S. S. Deutschland* occurred that inspired Hopkins' memorable poem.) Refusing to seek shelter from the gathering storm, Grimes points out the "grandeur in a gale of wind," but soon that wind ushers in a torrential rain that sends his apprentice plummeting to his death and ultimately leads to Peter's own demise when, through the fog of his mental breakdown, he realizes that self-destruction is his only way out of an impossible situation.

Even in present-day real life, people whose livelihoods bring them into intimate contact with nature must come to terms with its "both-sidedness." Environmentalist Bill McKibben, in *Wandering Home,* quotes his friend Chris Granstrom: "I have a much more complicated relationship with nature since I became a farmer. Things that seem benign or beautiful when they don't threaten you directly become something else. Like thunderstorms" (p. 34).

If, in Europe, artistic expression of nature's "dangerous" side first resulted from the popularity of travel and alpinism, in the young United States the phenomena that produced this consciousness were inherent in the territory. The drive to create a peculiarly American art led to a concentration on, and celebration of, its wilderness; intentionally scaling the peaks of the Catskills or the Adirondacks or the White Mountains looking for artistic subjects or even simply exploring the wilderness in one's own neighborhood entailed risks. The Hudson River School painter Thomas Cole (1801–49) was a tireless walker, rambling for hours and miles on end from his Catskill, New York, home in search of picturesque views to paint. In his journal he left a dramatic and romantic account of being overtaken by a thunderstorm during one of his mountain rambles. Cole broke one of the classic rules for wilderness safety: he ignored the approach of a threatening weather front, hoping the clouds would simply pass, and very suddenly found himself enveloped in deep darkness that soon gave way to an exceedingly violent display of thunder, lightning, rain, and wind. Taking shelter under a ledge of overhanging rock, he eventually noticed that he was trapped there by newly formed torrents, on each side of "his" rock, that "met a short distance below [him]; and thence plunged into the deep obscurity of the valley." He had just faced the likelihood of having to spend the night in this wind-and-rain-soaked prison, with nothing but the "niggard remnants of a former meal" in his backpack, when a final, fierce blast of wind tore the clouds apart and the storm ended as quickly as it had begun, "and [he] pursued [his] way down the mountain's side with a heart filled with delight."

Thus, it's not difficult to understand how Cole could relate to the natural disaster that befell a family in Crawford Notch, in the White Mountains of New Hampshire, two years before his first visit there. Today Route 302 takes you through Crawford Notch en route to the tourist mecca of North Conway. This is an impressive scenic drive with some pretty spots where you can pull over, get out for a walk, and even, if you wish, enjoy the amenities of the Appalachian Mountain Club's new visitor center. The awesomeness of the Notch—and thus a hint of its intimidating past—is most apparent from the top of Mt. Willard, an easily climbable peak at the northwest end of the Notch (I've been up Mt. Willard in a rainstorm). But in the nineteenth century, Crawford Notch had two rather fearful connotations. First, in the religious mind of the day, the Notch, with its erratic boulders perched high up on the mountains and cliffs, was believed to have been caused by Noah's flood. Second, it was the site of what has ever since been etched in the local psyche as the Willey Disaster. Cole, who on first seeing the place in 1828, wrote in his journal of "the horrors of that night [August 28, 1826]...when these mountains were deluged with rocks and trees were hurled from high places down the steep channeled sides of the mountains." On that tragic night, Samuel Willey, his wife, their five children, and two hired men were buried alive. "A dreadful mystery hangs over the events of that night," Cole continued. "...We looked up at the pinnacles above us and measured ourselves as nothing."

Returning to that area in 1839, Cole sketched out what became one of his best-known paintings, *A View of the Mountain Pass Called the Notch of the White Mountains* (also called *Crawford Notch*). He appears to have reconstructed the scene as it looked in the hours just prior to the disaster. The house is standing, and smoke curls from its chimney. A man and child have emerged to greet a man who approaches on horseback. At first glance, this is a scene of domestic rural tranquility—but one with a sense of foreboding. The horse rears up as if frightened by something. Storm clouds in the left of the painting are pouring torrential rains down on the mountains and are approaching the home.

The *Crawford Notch* was not only Cole's artistic response to the Willey Disaster but also his attempt to answer that haunting question: "Why? Where was God in this?" Cole and his contemporaries were no different from us. They asked, "Where was God?" and "Why the Willeys?" This was an upstanding, hardworking, moral family; the tragedy made no sense. Inevitably, as art historian Rebecca Bedell points out, "most interpreters were forced to fall back on the mysterious workings of God" (*The Anatomy of Nature,* 43). Fortunately, although the interpreters did look for moral lessons to be derived from such events, they fell short of declaring outright that God "caused" them.

Calvin Got It All Wrong

Attempts to subject God's role in nature's both-sidedness to the scrutiny of ironclad logic must necessarily lead to dire conclusions. To accept the logical implications of Calvin's doctrine of God's absolute sovereignty is to maintain that if God "wills" good, then God must also "will" evil. Yet, does this not fly in the face of our belief in an infinitely loving God? Or have we so far stretched the meaning of the word *love,* in our misguided insistence on applying it to abusive parents (and occasionally spouses) who "really love us but just don't know how to show it," that we're willing to project this perverted notion of love onto God as well? Msgr. George Denzer, one of my scripture professors in the seminary and a man of passionate opinions, told of attending the wake of a little girl who had been killed by a car, and hearing misguided people try to comfort the parents by telling them it was "God's will" that this should happen. What this saintly man had to say about such people is, in our politically correct age, unprintable.

On the face of it, the position that God "wills" only good but "permits" evil appears to create an unsatisfying dualism that raises more questions than it answers. However, Eastern Orthodox theologian David Bentley Hart—in his magisterial extended reflection *The Doors of the Sea: Where Was God in the Tsunami?*—offers a compelling refutation of Calvin's "absolute sovereignty" doctrine and an excellent theological rationale for God's both willing good while permitting evil. Indeed, Hart is quick to point out that Calvin's doctrine is not to be found in the New Testament and that no less an authority than Thomas Aquinas held strongly for a distinction between God's willing and God's permitting. Positing the existence of primary causality (willing) and secondary causality (permitting), Hart decries the forms of "theological fatalism" that fail to distinguish between the two and thereby "defame the love and goodness of God out of a...fascination with his 'dread sovereignty'" (89). This eloquent theologian could hardly have better scriptural support than the prophet Ezekiel, who says, "I have no pleasure in the death of anyone, says the Lord GOD. Turn, then, and live" (Ezek 18:32).

Human Agency

By now it must be obvious that prominent in my constellation of natural disasters are those that result when human beings consciously and deliberately insert themselves into close contact with nature, sometimes in potentially dangerous circumstances. (I write, after all, not so much as a theologian whose leisure activities are hiking and photography, but rather as a theologically trained hiker, scenic photographer, and cultural historian.) This raises the question of human agency in a big way. The poor souls who were swept away without warning by the tsunami of December 2004 can hardly be blamed because they happened to be sitting on a beach in Indonesia or, for some other reason, found themselves within drowning distance of the "mighty torrents and waves" that swept over them on that day of wrath. But what, for example, of the climbers up Everest, Denali, or even lesser peaks such as Mounts Hood or Washington, who set out on their quests despite dire warnings of bad weather?

In mountaineering or hiking accidents, or maritime incidents in which, perhaps, an inexperienced crew is a factor, it's easy enough to point the finger at human responsibility. Yet we are increasingly becoming conscious of human responsibility—or human complicity, in some cases—as contributing to such major disasters as earthquakes and hurricanes, the kind of event normally termed "acts of God." That awareness has been with us since at least the eighteenth century.

In 1755 an earthquake estimated to have reached 9.0 on the Richter scale struck Lisbon, Portugal, killing at least 60,000 people. The great French philosopher Voltaire composed a lengthy poem about the disaster, in which he delivered a scathing attack on what David Bentley Hart terms the "odd, bland metaphysical optimism" (17) that would claim this world is the best of all possible worlds and all things "happen for the best," according to some divine plan. Who could look upon such suffering and actually want to believe in a God whose "divine plan" included such tragedies?

Into the fray jumped Rousseau, Voltaire's contemporary. Reading Voltaire as wanting to shift the blame for the Lisbon tragedy from God to "dumb nature," Rousseau wrote him a letter noting that it wasn't "dumb nature" that had built the six- and seven-story houses that collapsed, and pointing out that many had died because they refused to leave Lisbon after the first shock waves occurred or insisted on returning to retrieve their belongings. Rousseau's point: Humans bear some of the responsibility for this tragedy.

Mark Silk, writing in the online journal *Religion in the News* ("Was New Orleans Asking for It?"), cites Rousseau as illustrating how the shift from simply blaming natural disasters on God to ascribing them to human failure began at this time. Silk notes that some historians mark this as the start of "a new conception in the world's moral economy—one that, on the occasion of natural disasters, evades the impulse to justify God by making humanity the agent of its own suffering. What is at issue, now, is not God's goodness and power but man's technical and moral capacity to prevent suffering." Nowhere in our present time is this more telling than with Hurricane Katrina, in whose wake human complicity has gradually come to light with regard to both prevention and mitigation. Fire heats our homes and fire can reduce our homes to ashes. Water cleanses and refreshes us and it can drown us. The same omnipotent Creator who established the physical laws that govern all these activities also gave human beings the intellectual capacity to discover those laws and, thus, to develop ways of predicting, or (perhaps) preventing, or mitigating the effects of certain natural disasters.

(It's interesting to note that Voltaire took his stance about natural disasters having no moral significance some seventy years *before* Thomas Cole and his contemporaries painstakingly searched for moral lessons in the Willey Disaster in New Hampshire. The Americans were likely influenced by the great Puritan divine Jonathan Edwards [1703–58] and the allegorical interpretations of natural phenomena that he set out in his influential *Images or Shadows of Divine Things;* although Cole, for one, clearly parted company with Edwards' thinking in many respects.)

Human agency frequently plays a crucial role in those harrowing instances of what Laurence Gonzales calls "deep survival." The stories he tells in his book of that title offer fertile territory in which to look for God.

There was Nick Williams, a business executive alone on a routine skiing trip, who became enveloped in a sudden blizzard, misread a map in his haste to forge a shortcut back to the ski lodge, and spent two nights outdoors, underdressed and with no food or water, in a relentless, utterly freezing storm. His mental toughness, developed during his Marine fighter pilot days and his ascent up the corporate ladder, allowed him to survive these impossible conditions.

Yachtswoman Debbie Kiley, the first woman to sail in the Whitbread Around the World race, once let herself be talked into being part of a crew of five that was to deliver a yacht from Maine to Florida. Kiley and her shipmate Brad Cavanagh, by disciplining themselves into a positive mental attitude while their colleagues succumbed to derangement and ultimately to sharks after their yacht sank in a hurricane, survived five days in a dinghy before a Russian freighter picked them up.

More recently there was Joe Simpson, hero of the memoir *Touching the Void,* who broke his leg 19,000 feet above sea level on the snow-covered, uninhabited Siula Grande, a mountain in the Peruvian Andes. The Scottish mountaineer managed to devise all sorts of ways to keep his body going and his mind alert until, astoundingly, he staggered into base camp at the very moment his climbing mate, who naturally had assumed that Simpson was dead, was preparing to depart.

In analyzing the dynamics of these and countless other stories of deep survival, Gonzales identifies qualities that literally make the difference between life and death in the outcomes of human encounter with natural disasters. Highest on the list of these qualities is self-control. Giving in to fear in a stressful situation hampers the rational thought needed to survive. Self-control, according to Gonzales, is the most important skill needed in survival situations, whether they involve skydiving or being stranded in the wilderness. "And with more and more novices going into the wilderness for fun," he observes, "the severe penalties that come with a failure of control are becoming evident in the increasing number of search and rescue operations that are launched to save them or recover their bodies" (38).

Closely related to self-control is allowing reason to take precedence over emotion. Whether one is a neophyte or an expert, this is vital in a survival situation: "Nature doesn't adjust to our level of skill," Gonzales points out (91).

Without a doubt, the insertion of human agency into the picture offers an entirely new dimension in which to look for God in natural disasters. Is God in the clear-headedness and courage that spurs those involved to find a way out, in face of their overwhelming fear? Is God in the sense of humor that allows them to see their situation in perspective? Or is God perhaps in the moment of insight when they *know* they are going to survive?—for, Gonzales points out, such a moment is common (if not universal) in these situations.

And who can forget the story of Aron Ralston, the twenty-seven-year-old who amputated his own arm when it became trapped under a rock when he went canyoneering on his own with no one knowing where he was? Far from having a clear insight that he was going to make it, Ralston was convinced that he was doomed, even going so far as to record final messages and his last will and testament with his video camera. Occasionally he would pray, but was never certain whether God was listening. Suddenly, long past the time when someone in his dire predicament should have expired, Ralston realized that his trapped arm, its circulation having been cut off for several days, was rotting. Not only would it never again be of any use to him, but the poisons generated by the process of decomposition would soon course through the rest of his body and kill him.

Ralston had already considered the theoretical possibility of amputating his arm as a means of escape, and had even made a half-hearted attempt at it, but he proved too squeamish to carry it through. Now the flash of insight that his dying arm was slowly killing him gave him the courage at last to do the necessary deed. And this is what finally saved him. Was this the decisive sign of God's presence? Could God be found in Ralston's basic survivor mentality?—for, despite his belief that he was going to die, he displayed all the survivor's instincts of thinking rationally, developing a routine, and even displaying a sense of humor on occasion, not least when he ran out of liquid and was reduced to drinking his own urine.

In the end, looking for God in natural disasters is not about facilely ascribing them to God's will; nor, certainly, is it about interpreting them as God's judgment upon whatever groups of people one happens to hate at the moment. Nor has it anything to do with offering pious platitudes about the positive benefit of suffering "because it motivates compassion," a position rejected by British theologian Tina Beattie in *The Tablet* immediately following the 2004 tsunami ("Where Was God?"). To adopt one of these positions is, after all, to claim to have *found* God, which is presumptuous indeed.

To talk about *looking for* God, on the other hand, is to acknowledge God's mystery. It's to accept that God can't be "found" as easily as you find a colored egg on Easter morning. I look for God among the amazing variety of human responses in the face of natural disasters and, above all, in the "both sides" of nature and in artists' attempts to come to terms, via their respective media, with that duality. To acknowledge God's mystery is to accept that we can't nail God down to our way of thinking about how God "should" act, and that we can't limit God to our notions of how God *does* act. In the end, both God and nature will always surprise us.

Questions for Reflection

1. In his great work of systematic theology, *The Institutes of the Christian Religion,* John Calvin unpacks, with a top-notch lawyer's closely reasoned arguments, the implications of his doctrine of God's sovereignty. Is logic the only possible response when faced with contemplating the place of God in nature's beauty? In nature's tragedies? Why or why not?

2. In the popular song from the sixties, Judy Collins sings that she has looked at clouds from both sides now, and yet it's clouds' illusions that she recalls; she really doesn't know clouds. Have you ever looked at nature from both sides? Did this present you with an illusion about God, or did you find that you ended up really knowing something about God?

3. Aron Ralston was virtually an accident waiting to happen. An avid, even obsessive adventurer, he was known for putting himself in dangerous situations long before the accident in which he lost his arm. How would you answer someone who claims that this canyoneering accident was God's judgment on him for being foolhardy?

Bibliography

Beattie, Tina. "Where Was God?" *The Tablet,* January 8, 2005, 8–9.

Bedell, Rebecca. *The Anatomy of Nature: Geology & American Landscape Painting, 1825–1875.* Princeton and Oxford: Princeton University Press, 2001.

Cole, Thomas. *The Collected Essays and Prose Sketches.* Edited by Marshall Tymn. St. Paul, MN: John Colet Press, 1980.

Cole, Thomas. *A View of the Mountain Pass Called the Notch of the White Mountains (Crawford Notch).* Two books in which this painting can be found are Matthew Baigell's *Thomas Cole,* New York: Watson-Guptill Publications, 1998; and Earl A. Powell's *Thomas Cole,* New York: Harry N. Abrams, 2000.

Edwards, Jonathan. *Images or Shadows of Divine Things.* Edited by Perry Miller. Repr. Westport, CT: Greenwood Press, 1977.

Gonzales, Laurence. *Deep Survival: Who Lives, Who Dies, and Why.* New York and London: W. W. Norton, 2004.

Hart, David Bentley. *The Doors of the Sea: Where Was God in the Tsunami?* Grand Rapids, MI, and Cambridge, UK: Wm. B. Eerdmans, 2005.

Gerard Manley Hopkins. Edited by Catherine Phillips. The Oxford Authors. Oxford and New York: Oxford University Press, 1986.

Kraus, Hans-Joachim. *Theology of the Psalms.* Minneapolis: Augsburg, 1986.

McKibben, Bill. *Wandering Home.* New York: Crown Publishing, 2005.

Ralston, Aron. *Between a Rock and a Hard Place.* New York: Simon & Schuster, 2005.

Silk, Mark. "Was New Orleans Asking for It?" *Religion in the News* 8, no. 2 (Fall 2005): 1, 25.

9

Appreciating the Beauty
A Traditional Hawaiian Tale
Robert Béla Wilhelm

Every winter I go to the Big Island of Hawaii and stay in the town of Hilo. Two tsunamis destroyed downtown Hilo in 1947 and 1962. The Pacific Tsunami Museum is one reminder; the evacuation-route markings on the streets are another. And then there are the ever-present loudspeakers and alarm systems dotting the town, threatening to bellow out early warning by day or by night.

Most local people have family stories about the tsunamis, and there is a general nervousness about earthquakes in far-off Alaska or Chile. They could deliver a huge tsunami to Hawaii's shores. The bottom of the condominium I rent is mounted on concrete and steel piers—to let a tsunami pass below the building the next time one crashes ashore.

But that is not the only fear. From the top of my condominium, I can see the volcanic ash and smoke billowing out of Pu'u O'o on the slopes of Mount Kilauea in Volcanoes National Park. In 1984 lava flowed down the slope stopping just a few miles from Hilo.

Amid the tranquil beauty of Hawaii there is the ever-present threat of a natural disaster. The ancient stories and myths of Hawaii tell us something important about living with possible cataclysms—even when the surroundings seem so idyllic, so peaceful, so safe.

There is something startling about how ancient traditional storytellers dealt with what we call today "natural disasters." For in the traditional world, there is nothing really "natural" about disasters. All around the world stories of natural calamities—Hawaii included—are transformed into creation and re-creation stories. The focus is never on the details of the outward events, but on the response of the human heart.

Our natural disasters, according to traditional storytellers, have three distinct aspects: divine action, human response, and an "outbursting" of physical display within the material world.

First, there is divine action. Disasters are seen not as the work of God but as an occasion for God to work with the chaos and make of it a new creation. God is neither the First Cause—nor even the "First Responder"—to natural disasters. Instead, God is the *ultimate* responder who will bring new life out of the chaos of death.

Second, there is the role of humanity in all cataclysms. In a sense, there is no disaster unless humans experience it, interpret it, and cope with it. Are we humans responsible, and how? Do we sometimes in our actions, or failures to act, provoke or magnify a natural disaster?

The before and the after of a cataclysm are the occasions for our human response. And these responses are rarely morally neutral. Our actions are noble or despicable. They are good or bad. They are creative or destructive.

Finally, there are the forces of nature—acting with a seemingly vast indifference to the consequences, but with traumatic impact. Oceanic storms swallowing ships and shorelines, torrents of floodwaters descending the mountains, firestorms raging across great forests, and deadly blizzards blowing across the open plains: all seem to proclaim nature's indifference to human life. Yet, divine, human, and natural elements all participate in the great cataclysms. How do we explain their interdependence? How do we gain solace in the face of disaster and loss?

Let me tell you a traditional Hawaiian tale about a natural disaster, which illustrates the divine, human, and natural dimensions to cataclysmic events:

I usually arrive in Hawaii early in the winter, before the first snow has fallen on Hawaii's tallest mountain, Mauna Kea. What excitement to awake in the morning and to get a glimpse of the great snowcap hovering 13,000 feet above the tropical shoreline! It seems so strange: the mountaintop is the only place in warm, tropical Hawaii that is not teeming with life. A cold mantle of snow covers one small part of this lush paradise.

As I admire the beauty of Mauna Kea, I always think about the old Hawaiian story that described how that snowcap was once the only part of Hawaii that was not destroyed by a natural disaster. The story reverses the way we normally see Hawaii, for in the tale most of the island is destroyed. But the most remote and desolate part of it—the mountaintop—is the source of new life. Here is the story:

Long ago the Hawaiian Islands were created out of the sea and given an abundance of blessings. And the people who lived there enjoyed these blessings in many ways. Fish were plentiful, and the land was lush with fruit. The seasons were gentle, and there was both rain and sunshine. And every day there were *anuenue*—rainbows—that played in the sky in the places between the sun and the rain.

So the people built places where they could give thanks for their many gifts. They built great *heiaus*—stone temples—from the lava rock. Those temples by the sea were frequently dedicated to the sharks who were the guardians of the water. The fishermen brought gifts to the *pohaku*—the sacred stones—that each had close to his house and his boat. These were dressed with leis—strings of tropical flowers or seashells. Other gifts were fresh fruit or small offerings of food wrapped in banana or taro leaves.

...And so the story begins with a description of the cosmos as it should be. It is a creation, and the realities of divinity, humanity, and nature are all linked together. This is a picture of the ideal community, the ideal town, the ideal family that we all imagine and long for. But even as we listen to the words of the storyteller, we know that this harmony will not prevail. What will break the link?

Since this is a human story, we naturally look to ourselves.

Now, the modern reader may recoil at the next episode, thinking it is simply blame-making. But remember, in the traditional world there is not a slavish following of the principles of cause and effect. Rather, there is a sense of synchronicity: When something goes wrong in the heavens, or on the earth, or in the underworld, it may well be happening simultaneously elsewhere. The natural world mirrors us, as we mirror God.

And so, to return to the story...

The people of Hawaii came to forget the ways of thankfulness they had learned from ancient times. They no longer gave offerings of thanks and praise for their abundance. Now the *heiaus* were deserted, and the lava-rock walls began to crumble. The *pohaku* were no longer draped with leis, and were no longer offered food wrapped in leaves. All the food was eaten by the people themselves.

...Here the story is describing how creation ebbs away into chaos if there is no constant vigilance. In Christian terms, we might consider the vivid images (paraphrased below) from Luke 21:34–36: "Watch out! Or your hearts will harden and the day of doom will spring upon you suddenly.... Stay awake! Pray constantly. And stand tall before the coming of the Son of Man!"

Now, listen to the continuation of the Hawaiian tale...

There was a certain fisherman who lived on the beach of Kawaihae. He lived near the great *heiau* dedicated to the Shark Guardians. But no one ever went there any more to sing *Mele*—sacred chants—or to dance the hula in gratitude for the gifts of creation. The fisherman did not do these things either. He also neglected the *pohaku* by his hut. It was now overturned, and mostly hidden by the drifting sand.

Early every morning the fisherman set out to sea without any thankfulness in his heart. And he returned by nightfall without any song of joy and praise on his lips. Like all the others, he too had forgotten thankfulness.

Though he worked hard, his catch was meager. Most of it went to the house of the chieftain. And so the fisherman grumbled as he paddled his boat away from Kawaihae to the fishing grounds while it was still dark. As he labored, the stars slowly disappeared, and the sky grew lighter. Then the sun rose above the peak of Mauna Kea—the White Mountain—which was snowcapped during the winter months. But the fisherman did not stop to behold its beauty.

All day he worked as the sun crossed the sky. And he worked even as it sank into the deep sea in the west. He never stopped to see the green flash that momentarily danced on the horizon at sunset. And so he did not see the beauty that was before him.

...Let me stop the tale here and tell you a little of my experience in Hawaii. There is a small outdoor donut shop just north of Hilo. The donuts—*malasadas,* as they are called locally—are the best on the Big Island. I frequently stop there just as the sun comes up, usually to find a local man, Andy, sitting at the outdoor table, holding a coffee cup, and waiting for the first *malasadas* to be brought out of the shop by Komo the baker.

"Did you ever see anything more beautiful than this, Bob?" he would say to me, gesturing with his free hand toward the warm pink sky toward the east. "The sun comes up every day. And every day is a beautiful day. There's nothing that I can do to make it happen. But I can be thankful. I can appreciate the Beauty."

Hawaiians have a strong sense of the fragility of their little island world. But they assert mastery over this fragility by celebrating beauty. Like goodness, like truth, beauty affirms creation over chaos. And if the "Beauty" is not appreciated, if it is taken for granted, then a dulling of the mind and a hardening of the heart follow. Then storm waves begin to beat upon the shore, the earth quakes with volcanic activity, and the pressure of the hot lava builds into an explosive anger.

Let me return to the old Hawaiian tale...

One morning the fisherman caught nothing, and by noon he raised his voice in anger, shouting aloud from the loneliness of his boat:

"Where is justice? Where are my fish? Where are the Guardians of the Sea who withhold my catch? Oh! There is no divinity. There is only human misery!"

By the time he was finished cursing, he was standing upright in his boat with his clenched fist shaking in anger at the still and silent sea. With that, the sky darkened and a strong wind stirred the waves. And out of the depths came a great blue shark, baring its rows and rows of teeth, and saying:

"Fisherman! We give you no fish because you are no longer thankful. You and others have all become wicked, and have neglected the *heiaus* dedicated to us.

"And now, you even doubt our existence and you curse us!"

...In Western culture, the shark is a terrifying image, and so we do not appreciate the ambivalent nature of this epiphany to the Hawaiian fisherman. The shark can also be a protecting spirit. Indeed, its body— *Kino* in Hawaiian—can be the form taken by both humans and gods. The shark, like the natural disaster it sometimes portends, provokes both fear and awe, both terror and grace...

The fisherman was astonished and fearful, but at that moment he no longer doubted. He fell to his knees and lowered his head.

The Great Blue Shark continued:

"Therefore, we shall now flood all these islands to cleanse them of all human life—Hawai'i, Maui, Moloka'i, and all the other islands as well."

The fisherman was frightened and began to beg forgiveness. He promised to pray daily, and to offer generous gifts at the altar. His anger was spent, and now his heart was filled with regret. And then, the fisherman wept, and his tears—the tears in his eyes—came from his heart.

Robert Béla Wilhelm

…The ancient Hawaiian storyteller is presenting us with difficult truths as he speaks to our own hearts. But our minds protest and refuse the message. Our minds say: "It is not fair that all the islands should be destroyed." But the mind is more crafty than wise, and realizing that this argument will fail, the mind begins to bargain: "But if all must be destroyed, at least save one. Save *me*. I am sorry." And with these words the mind falters, for sorrow dwells elsewhere than the mind. And so the heart begins to speak. And the heart prefers its own vocabulary. Where words once sprang forth, tears now flow.

Now, to return to the ancient tale…

The Shark Guardian remained motionless; its great head arose out of the water just a short distance from the little boat. When the fisherman looked up again, the Shark no longer seemed terrible.

Instead, the Shark looked sad. The Guardian had pity and said:

"Fisherman, I cannot take back my word, but I will hold the waters back from the very, very top of Mauna Kea. Climb to the top with your wife, and you two will be spared. Now, hurry!"

And they fled the beach at Kawaihae, taking nothing with them. They ran through the scrub of the Keawe trees in the lowlands, up to the forests where the Ohia and Koa trees grew. And then they climbed beyond the forests to the barren rock ground of Mauna Kea's high slopes.

Mauna Kea was covered with snow. The fisherman and his wife were cold and tired and hungry. It took them three days to reach the mountain summit.

Then a great puffy wall of billowy clouds blew in from the west, like the coming of the first winter storm. And a wall of water followed.

The fisherman and his wife saw it engulf all the coastal villages.

The great tidal wave flooded the high mountain-villages and the taro patches. Next the wave swallowed the great trees of the forest, and soon the wave was cresting as it approached the summit. There it stopped, leaving only a small snowy outcropping, a little white island, for the fisherman and his wife. But all the Hawaiian Islands were now under the sea.

…Let me stop the story for a moment, and describe what can be seen on the Big Island today. Throughout Hawaii there are modern-day *pohaku*—small standing stones that visitors and tourists often fail to see. One might be a solitary stone arising out of a sandy beach, another a mostly submerged stone placed at the base of a waterfall, still another a

121

stone tentatively perched on a cliffside or volcanic rim. Atop all these are small gifts of gratitude—a flower, a seashell, a piece of fruit, or even a trinket or a few small coins.

In the same way, a Great *Pohaku* was all that remained of Mauna Kea when the flood waters drowned the rest of the mountain. And this Great *Pohaku* also held an offering. The Hawaiian storytellers created this image in the hearts of their listeners: for at the top of this *pohaku* there are two creatures of incomparable beauty—the Fisherman and the Fisherwife. They lifted up their hearts and offered them in beauty and in gratitude. Now, to continue with my tale...

The flood waters beat against the rocky summit for ten days and for ten nights. And then the water receded. All life on Hawaii was destroyed, except for the fisherman and his wife.

They climbed down the cold mountains, and across the uplands, and finally down to the warm beach where they gave thanks among the ruins of one of the temples. They made leis from the seaweed and draped a stone *pohaku* as they prayed together.

Then the man and the woman gathered shellfish and ate. When the rains came, they drank the sweet waters that came down from Mauna Kea to Kawaihae and flowed out to the sea.

And from that day onwards, the fisherman and the fisherwife walked the path of righteousness.

Every day they saw rainbows—*anuenue*—in the sky, halfway between the rain and the sun. And whatever else they were doing, they stopped to marvel at the beauty. And to give thanks.

Life returned to the land, and children were born to the couple. The *heiau* and *pohaku* were tended with care, the crops grew, and the fish were plentiful. Out of the chaos came a new Creation.

...And so my story ends. Many tourists who come to the Big Island, and stay on the Kona side, drift to the beaches at sunset to watch for the famous "green flash" as the sun sinks into the sea. But I prefer to keep vigil just before the sun comes up on the Hilo side. And while the sun is still hidden from my eyes by the watery horizon, I turn toward the mountain and see the first shaft of light strike snowcapped Mauna Kea. The icy white top is bathed in a warm pink light. I see the dawn of Creation. I see the Beauty.

Did you enjoy the story? Here are some questions to think about:

1. Have I ever experienced the power and beauty of nature and yet feared the danger? Have I ever sensed that Creation could dissolve into chaos, that Beauty could be destroyed by danger?
2. How is it to pick up the pieces after a storm, a blizzard, a flood, a fire, a tornado? Do I only see what was lost? Or can I imagine what will be reborn?
3. Did my lack of vigilance and preparedness make a natural disaster even more dangerous for me or others? Did I ever regret failing to help during a disaster, or immediately afterward, when I could have helped?
4. Am I more likely to experience despair or paralysis during a disaster? Or am I likely to experience determination to survive and even thrive in the face of a calamity?